HAPPY STORIES!

REAL-LIFE INSPIRATIONAL STORIES
FROM AROUND THE WORLD
THAT WILL RAISE YOUR HAPPINESS LEVEL

HAPPY STORIES!

REAL-LIFE INSPIRATIONAL STORIES
FROM AROUND THE WORLD
THAT WILL RAISE YOUR HAPPINESS LEVEL

Will Bowen

Published by Grand Harbor Press

www.apub.com

Amazon, the Amazon logo, and Grand Harbor Press are
trademarks of Amazon.com, Inc., or its affiliates.

ISBN-13: 9781477848241

ISBN-10: 147784824X

Cover design by Ray Cashbaugh

Cover images ©2013 Shutterstock Images LLC

Library of Congress Control Number: 2013910361

Printed in the United States of America

DEDICATION

For Marti—my breath is
yours, and yours is mine.

CONTENTS

INTRODUCTION

A happy life consists not in the absence, but in the mastery of hardships.
—Helen Keller

Welcome to Happiness!

Three years ago, I set out on an adventure—an adventure to unravel the mysteries of happiness.

What I discovered is that happiness is the result of the way we think, speak, and act. These three things combine to form our habits, character, and destiny. Our highest destiny is to be happy.

Nearly one hundred thousand copies of *Happy This Year!* have sold around the world in just the first few months of publication. The lessons in *Happy This Year!* can be applied by themselves or magnified with the HappyStat app, which is available online wherever apps are sold for your smartphone or other device and at our website: www.HappyStoriesBook.com.

Happy Stories! is a collection of real stories about real people who have figured out how to be happy.

In *Happy Stories!* you will meet parents, businesspeople, entrepreneurs, students, retirees, construction workers, nonprofit directors, yoga teachers, high school principals, stay-at-home moms, artisans, and individuals from other walks of life—all of whom have two things in common.

1. They tend to be exceptionally happy
2. Their happiness impressed other people so much that they were nominated for inclusion in this series

When I began following up on leads and interviewing happy people, I wondered if they were upbeat simply because they had somehow sidestepped major challenges and had been spared the harsh realities of life.

What I discovered was that the opposite is more often true. The people whose stories you will read have *not* lived idyllic lives. If anything, they have had more than their share of hardships.

I've asked each of them to share their suggestions for happiness. You'll read their comments at the end of their story, but as you read you'll note certain common themes in *all* of the stories. One, we've already discussed:

> *Happy people are not people without problems; they are people who face their problems and at some point make a decision to move past them.*

You will see that nearly all of these happy individuals have experienced some *major* difficulty, and rather than avoid their tribulations or wallow in their misery, they each made a decision to accept their situation and move on.

Another theme key to all of the stories is:

> *Happy people define themselves as being happy.*

Whenever someone was nominated, we would call that person, explain the reason for our call, and then ask if he or she was happy. Without exception, happy people are comfortable and confident in defining themselves as being happy. Their responses were, typically, some variation of:

"Absolutely!"

"Me? I'm very happy."

"Yes, I'm happy. I choose to be happy, so I am."

And therein lies the other theme shared by each of these stories:

Happy people choose to be happy.

Without exception, every one of these happy people made a conscious decision to be happy regardless of the problems or challenges they endured. They each made a commitment to take control of their own level of happiness and not allow it to be dictated by others or by life's circumstances.

Joining the ranks of happy people isn't difficult. They are always thrilled to expand their numbers. You simply have to begin to shift your way of thinking so that you start to see life, with both its exciting discoveries *and* its heartbreaking experiences, as a happy person would.

The happy people you will meet in *Happy Stories!* are more than inspirational; they are great teachers who have broken the code to happiness and who are both willing and excited to share that information with you.

Begin to follow their example, and, who knows, someone may soon recommend you as being a shining example of what it means to live a truly happy life.

If you wish to learn more about the people featured in this book and see their photos, nominate a happy person, learn more about happiness, download the free HappyStat smartphone app, or connect with me, visit www.HappyStoriesBook.com.

Here's to your happiness!

Will Bowen
Will@HappyStoriesBook.com

LAUGHING ALL THE WAY TO HAPPINESS

A man from the Midwest discovers the power of happiness through shared laughter.

We must laugh before we are happy.

—Jean de La Bruyère

T he midnight-blue van glided smoothly to a stop in an empty parking space. The driver took a deep breath and switched off the lights, letting the engine idle while he and his passenger sat silently in the dark.

"Are you sure this is the right place?" he asked.

"I think so," she replied, glancing about anxiously.

The choice of the location was not arbitrary. The timing was intentional. Everything was carefully and exactingly preselected and planned to have the maximum impact—a busy grocery store in the middle of town during the height of after-work shopping.

"Do you see anyone else from our team?" she asked nervously.

"It's hard to say," he replied. "The place is packed."

A woman walked by pushing a cart full of groceries. Her young son clung to the front of the cart, swaying back and forth while singing a song from a recent Disney movie, his blond hair tousled by the breeze. The boy smiled broadly as he looked into the van; its occupants averted their eyes and remained still so as not to draw attention to themselves.

"Are we sure this is going to work?" he whispered.

"I'm not sure of anything," she replied. "You can back out if you want, but I'm in."

If shoppers had thought to check the calendar, they might not have been so surprised by what was about to go down. The significance of the date was right there for everyone to see. But, as often happens, things tend to become obvious only in retrospect.

"Let's go," he said, heaving open the van door. She leapt out and walked beside him, trying to stay close to him, but not too close. They wanted to look like ordinary shoppers just stopping by to pick up some groceries on their way home. Their plan required them to be clandestine, so they did their best to blend in.

As the pair entered the store, they saw their leader standing near the checkout line pretending to read a magazine. Seeing him, they felt a renewed commitment to their mission, but they also felt an increased uncertainty. Any second now the clock would strike 6:00 p.m., there would be an announcement, and then, well, then there would be an explosion—one that would affect the lives of hundreds of people.

They moved to their assigned places, seeing other accomplices in theirs as well. They pretended to scan shelves for food items.

Seconds later, the store's PA system crackled to life. They heard the announcement calling them into action, and then, just as they had been trained, they let loose—with laughter. For fifteen minutes, volunteers placed strategically around the store, exploded with laughter.

Soon, bystanders also began to laugh. First one, and then another, and then groups of people all joined in the laughter. The store manager found himself laughing, red-faced with tears streaming down his cheeks as he randomly hugged customers.

A laughter flash mob had successfully helped people forget their problems and take just a few moments to feel the happiness-inducing power of laughter.

This laughter flash mob was the brainchild of Patrick Sterenchuk, a certified Laughter Yoga instructor, and it took place the Monday before World Laughter Day, which began in 1998 in Mumbai, India, and is observed on the first Sunday of each May.

Even though the strategically placed laughter yogis caused a ripple of laughter to echo through a Dubuque, Iowa, Hy-Vee, it was not their intention to incite laughter. Patrick says, "We were not there to make anyone else laugh. We were simply there to nurture and nourish other people through laughter."

It worked. Several shoppers went up to Patrick to thank him for the experience, including a teacher who said, "Thank you! Today was a pretty intense day at school and now I feel great— thank you so much!"

Laughter yoga was created by Dr. Madan Kataria who years later would also establish World Laughter Day. While attempting to write an article on laughter for a renowned medical journal, Dr. Kataria suffered severe writer's block that caused him not only a great deal of frustration but insomnia as well.

After yet another sleepless night, Dr. Kataria took an ambling stroll through his hometown of Mumbai, savoring the morning twilight. In time, Dr. Kataria found himself in a city park, where he began to talk to random strangers about the link between laughter and emotional well-being.

Five of the men he spoke with got into the spirit of Dr. Kataria's work and began to gather around telling jokes. Soon, the entire group was erupting with laughter. They all noticed how much happier they felt as a result of their jokes and laughter and agreed to meet in the same park again the following morning.

The group grew to nearly fifty people in the coming weeks. However, a shift began to take place. As those gathered began to feel more comfortable with one another, the jokes began to take a turn toward being off-color and insensitive. A couple of people told Dr. Kataria that they were increasingly uncomfortable and would have to stop attending the morning laugh fests.

The next day, Dr. Kataria suggested that everyone simply look into one another's eyes and laugh without telling any jokes to get them started. At first, the laughter was forced, halting, but soon it transformed into peels of genuine and contagious laughter. Everyone left feeling elated and happy, and Dr. Kataria knew he was onto something—something special that has now spread around the world.

Patrick explains, "Some people call it fake laughter, but I don't resonate with that description. It's not fake—it's *intentional*. It's real laughter; it just starts without a joke or other catalyst. It's laughter for laughter's sake, and it leads to elevated levels of happiness because it lowers blood pressure, deepens breathing, and releases endorphins into the bloodstream."

Patrick has become somewhat famous in Dubuque. A self-described puck, Patrick helps people lighten up and enjoy life more. He's one of those guys you notice right away when he comes into a room. Not because of his beard, long hair, and tendency to wear long, flowing shawls, but because he pulsates with happy and positive energy. When he looks into your eyes, you feel a shift in your own experience of life. You sense that living is not the struggle you tend to think it to be but, rather, a comedic play that is to be savored, enjoyed, and never taken seriously.

Yoga—whether it's Laughter Yoga or any other type—is something that one practices. You will hear yogis refer to their practice when speaking of their yoga regimen because yoga is something that one is always tweaking, always seeking to improve and expand. The same is true for happiness.

Below, Patrick offers three suggestions, that if practiced on a consistent basis, can raise your level of happiness.

1. **Give yourself an energy boost:** Many people hit an energetic lull in the mid-afternoon, so they eat a sugary snack or down an energy drink to compensate. Patrick reminds us that the body has vast energy reserves that we can bring out through laughter.

   Schedule an energy boost every day at 2:00 p.m. First, laugh intentionally for thirty seconds. At first, you'll find this may feel a little forced and awkward, but stay with it. Then, for sixty seconds take long, slow deep breaths.

   Repeat this process three to five times. You will find that you feel lighter, happier, and more energetic, and that the benefits will last for several hours.

2. **Invitations not obligations:** Our expectations of other people can be a big drain on our emotions. When we ask someone to do something or, worse, have a belief that someone *should* do something and insist that he or she comply, it places a great stress on us. And the other person, noting

our anxiety and insistence that they conform to our expectations, may actually become *less* inclined to respond as we would like.

Instead, consider everything you want someone else to do to be an invitation that the other person may or may not choose to accept. Of course, if you are an employer or a parent who is trying to ensure a child's safety, you must have parameters and ground rules. Everyone else, however, should be released from the obligation of doing, being, living, and acting as you feel they should.

Patrick says that when he is dealing with other people, he will often chant "invitations not obligations" over and over in his mind.

3. **There is no vanity in the presence of gratitude:** Many people aren't as happy as they might be because they feel unappreciated, and yet there is a strong tendency in our culture to shrug off appreciation when it is offered. You may, like most people, have a tendency to deflect appreciation.

   When someone tells you how great you are, accept it—soak it in, know that you deserve it. Patrick says, "I see people almost apologizing for being awesome! My dad used to say, 'mediocrity hates greatness.' Maybe you being great makes some people angry, but it might be the catalyst to make them think, "I can do that, too.""

   According to Patch Adams—the real-life doctor depicted in the Robin Williams movie of the same name—children laugh four hundred times per day on average, whereas adults laugh only seventeen times per day. As we grow older, we lose the exuberant happiness of childhood. By following Patrick's suggestions, you can reclaim the happiness you had as a child and live happily every day.

HAPPINESS ROLLS ON

A teenager paralyzed in a motor vehicle accident goes on to live a happy, successful, and inspirational life.

Some people are walking around with full use of their bodies and they're more paralyzed than I am.

—Christopher Reeve

Thursday morning, August 26, 1976, 6:27 a.m.

Fwang! Fwang! Fwang!

"Ya hear that?" asked Ben.

Fwang! Fwang!

"Yeah, I hear it," Dale grouchily replied as he leaned over the steering wheel and squinted into the fog.

"*That's* the stop sign," said Ben. "See? It's right outside my window. I'm hitting it with my hand." *Fwang! Fwang!*

"So what?" spat Dale.

"So, it means that we're *at* the intersection. Right across this road we'll pick up Highway 224, and that'll take us to the job site," Ben said, continuing to slap the stop sign with his right palm.

"I can't see a damn thing," muttered Dale. "This fog is so thick I can't even see the stupid stop sign you're hitting—and *stop hitting the damn thing!*"

"Oooh . . . somebody's in a mood," Ben said, giving the sign one more big smack.

"Whatsamatter?" Ben sarcastically asked. "Didn't ya get enough beauty sleep last night, or are you still pissed about not being able to get the eight-track to work?"

Dale ignored the sarcastic salvo. Breathing deeply, he pressed the pedal softly and eased the pickup into the intersection.

Dale checked left, then right. Then, just to be safe, he looked left one more time.

"What the . . ." he shouted. They weren't there two seconds before, but now two large, round silver-white orbs were breaking out of the fog, shining into his eyes, and growing quickly closer. A horn blared that shook them in their seats.

"Christ!" screamed Dale as he stomped the accelerator.

But it was too late. The 18-wheeler slammed into the pickup, spinning it into a field. The pickup whirled around and around, and the force of the impact threw Dale and Ben around the cab like lotto balls.

Ben lost consciousness, awoke, and looked down to see his body splattered with blood—Dale's blood. Then his mind shut down.

Ben came to again, although he wasn't sure he was awake. He felt like he was still floating in a dream. He heard the sound of drilling and looked up into his father's eyes.

How long have I been asleep? he wondered. *My dad looks twenty years older.*

"They're drilling holes into your head to put you in traction," Ben's father said, caressing his cheek.

"Dale?" Ben's voice croaked.

"He's going to be fine."

The veil of unconsciousness covered Ben once more.

Ben had turned fifteen that summer. His father was proud to have given him his first job, working for him at his construction company. Ben and his dad were more than father and son; they were buddies, amigos. Ben loved working for his dad and hanging around with the other workers, all of whom were much older than he.

Being with rough-cut guys like Dale, sixteen years his senior, made Ben feel like a man, and his father reinforced Ben's adulthood at every turn, granting him responsibility while expecting accountability. He didn't cut Ben any slack just because he owned the company and Ben was his son.

Earlier that morning, Bennie Conley II, Ben's dad, had laid down the law with Ben. "I want the tools delivered to the site this morning so we can start the job tomorrow."

"We can just take 'em with us tomorrow," Ben said dismissively.

"No," said Bennie. "Do it today." Then he added wryly, "You realize today is payday, right? I'd hate to dock you for insubordination."

It was because of Bennie's prodding and gentle threat that Ben and Dale found themselves in the pickup truck that morning at the fog-shrouded intersection. It was because of Bennie's insistence that the task at hand be completed per his instructions that his son found himself lying in a hospital bed.

Bennie's grief was inconsolable. "It's my fault," he repeated over and over.

"It's called a hangman's break," the doctor explained when Ben finally awoke in the hospital. "You have what's known as a C2/C3 incomplete injury to the spine. It's what a hangman attempts to do to break the neck of a condemned criminal so that he will lose all neurological pathways to his lungs, heart, and vital organs and die quickly."

The doctor paused for questions. None came.

Bennie sat silently listening, the crushing weight of guilt pressing him into his chair.

"However," the doctor continued, "your spine didn't sever. That's why it's called incomplete. Actually, you're lucky."

Ben didn't feel lucky.

"You can breathe," said the doctor. "That's a good sign."

"When will I walk, doc?" he asked.

"That's hard to say," replied the doctor. Then, noticing the forlorn look on both Ben and Bennie's faces, he added, "Tell you what, kid. You work on getting better, okay? When you can wiggle your toes, that's when I'll tell you when you can walk."

Two months later, nurses were propping Ben up and pushing him around the grounds of Akron General in a wheelchair. Being out of the hospital gave him a renewed sense of hope and confidence. But then there was a setback.

"It's a pressure sore," said the nurse. "It's on your tailbone, and it comes from you not being able to move. We can't risk infection, so you're going to have to go back to bed until it heals."

"How long?" Ben asked. "Couple of days?"

The nurse smiled, "No, sweetheart. More like a week or two."

Ben was crestfallen. He was finally getting out of the bed, and now they were putting him back. He felt like Lazarus being re-entombed. He had come nowhere close to wiggling his toes or moving anything else below his neck for that matter.

Ben began to cry. His weeping became louder and more sustained until soon he was shouting. The nurses tried to console him, to no avail. Ben's yelling became filled with curses. He screamed at the top of his lungs, cursing everyone he could think of. He went at it for nearly four hours, until his throat was raw and his voice became hoarse.

The nurses sealed Ben's door in an attempt to mute the noise, but he was too loud. Desperate, the hospital sent a security guard into Ben's room. The guard told Ben that he would have to be quiet because he was scaring everyone in the hospital.

"Hit me!" Ben screamed.

"What?" the guard stammered.

"Take out your billy club and hit me! Hit me in the head! Hit me! Kill me! I can't live in this bed for the rest of my life!"

The guard stared down at his shoes. He could feel a knot forming in his throat. "Uh, listen, kid . . ."

"SHOOT ME!" demanded Ben. "You've got a gun. Pull it out and put a bullet through my brain! C'mon, *please,* kill me!"

All told, Ben screamed for nearly six hours until he passed out from exhaustion. He fell into a fitful and mournful sleep.

When Ben awoke the next morning, he saw that nothing had changed. He was still in the same bed and in the same room. He was still paralyzed below the neck.

As the morning dawned, something dawned within Ben as well. Nothing had changed, so Ben made a decision to change the only thing he could: *himself.* At this decision, a wave of peace broke over him. Ben's resentment for his situation melted, and he found himself aglow with appreciation—not because of what had happened to him, but for simply being alive.

Ben reflected on his situation and made new choices. He thought of what he had heard others say over the previous couple of months: "No one has ever lived with a C2/C3 spinal injury. . . ."

Well, I'm going to show them, Ben thought. *Not only am I going to live, I'm going to thrive.*

Ben knew that his father harbored immense guilt for what had happened and blamed himself. *I can't change what happened*, Ben thought, *But I can show Dad that even though my life has shifted, I can be happy and productive.*

That was thirty-eight years ago. Ben not only lived, he met a beautiful woman, and she has been his bride and best friend for more than fourteen years. Ben says, "It meant so much to my dad that I met Robin and fell in love, he got ordained from one of those mail-order places you see advertised on the back of *Rolling Stone* magazine, and he married us himself!"

"I'm one of the happiest people I know," Ben says, and below is his advice for maintaining a high level of happiness.

1. **Everyone has a disability—mine just shows:** Most people who can stand, walk, and move around are, nonetheless, paralyzed by fear, and so they don't attempt what they could do if they just tried.

   "I grew up in Virginia Beach, Virginia," says Ben. "I'd go out every day and help the lifeguards put out beach chairs and umbrellas in exchange for the free use of a raft. Then I'd spend all day riding the waves. After the accident, I thought I'd never get to do that again.

   "Then one day in 1987, my brother and my uncle took me out into the ocean. They held onto me as I bobbed up and down in the surf like a cork. A minute or so later, they let me go and a giant wave swept me tumbling to shore. It was exhilarating! Here I was, unable to move my body, and yet I could still bodysurf! I floated in the tide until they came and dragged me back out to do it again.

"Before my accident," Ben continues, "I used to ride motorcycles. One day, some friends lashed my limp body to the back of a Harley with an electrical cord and took me for a spin for forty-five minutes. I just kept shouting, 'go faster!'

"I bodysurf and ride motorcycles because I'm not afraid. I may be a quadriplegic, but it seems that other people are the ones who are paralyzed—by fear."

2. **Look for something beautiful every day:** "When I wake up in the morning, I set an intention to see something beautiful. I am going to scan the world around me until I can say, 'There, now *that* is truly beautiful.'

"I've been doing this for years, and the world has never failed to show me something spectacular. Why, just the other day I sat and watched the sunrise—I didn't just glance at the sky and appreciate the dawn, I really watched the whole process for more than an hour. First, the sky began to glow softly, and then the sun peered over the horizon. I could hear the birds begin to sing—just a few at first and then a whole chorus of birds all chirping and singing. I watched as the shadows of night withdrew, and then I felt the warmth of the sun on my face. It was incredible!

"People who are ambulatory tend to get so busy that they don't notice all of the beauty around them. I hate the saying 'Stop and smell the roses' because it's so trite, but it's also very true."

3. **Give yourself to others:** "I volunteer with the USO as well as with hospice. When you give your time to others, you stop focusing on yourself and your problems. Nothing makes you

feel better than helping others. That's one of the real keys to happiness."

When we read a story like Ben's, it's easy to be touched and inspired. However, it's far more important to follow his example. We should strive not to let fear paralyze us, we should look for something beautiful every day, and we should give ourselves to others.

Ben Conley's example shows us that happiness is what we do with our minds; it's not what we can or can't do with our bodies.

A Note from the Author

One week after Ben's story was first released in the serialized Kindle edition of this book, Ben Conley exhaled his last breath in this world and drew his first breath in the next. It's as if his spirit were waiting until his story was safely shared so that he could leave his paralyzed body and enter into his fully whole spirit body.

Heaven got a little happier the day Ben arrived.

SOARING WITH HAPPINESS

A man shares a unique way to resolve problems and discovers a powerful component of happiness in the process.

When once you have tasted flight, you will forever walk the earth with your eyes turned skyward, for there you have been, and there you will always long to return.
—Leonardo da Vinci

W here the hell is he going?" the young machine operator asked.

"To fix the machine," responded a seasoned coworker with a wry smile.

"But the machine is right here," insisted the young man. "He's walking toward the break room!"

"Exactly," said his colleague.

Charlie Mitchell and his maintenance team had spent the better part of an hour unsuccessfully working to repair a machine that flattened heated steel into sheets. At Charlie's suggestion, they all stopped trying and walked away.

"This is no time for a coffee break!" the young worker shouted to the departing group of men. "This thing's got to get up and running—now! We're getting behind. Everything is going to shut down behind us, and there'll be hell to pay!"

Charlie heard the young man's invectives, but he kept walking. If anything, the young man's urgency seemed to slow Charlie's pace, which was already quite slow. Charlie is a short, stocky man with a thick chest and arms that seem to dangle at his sides as he walks. With his beard, round teddy bear face, and side-to-side gait, some people have told Charlie that he resembles an Ewok—one of the hairy little characters from *Return of the Jedi.*

Such comments don't bother Charlie. In fact, it seems that nothing bothers him. Charlie is content in his life and his way of being. He is happy, and his happiness doesn't shift based on circumstances or comments from other people.

"But how is he going to fix the machine from the break room?" the worker demanded.

"Charlie says that most problems can be fixed with a cup of coffee. And I guess he's right. Since he's been the head of maintenance, the mill has never run so smoothly. If Charlie wants to stop working on something and have a cup of coffee, then that's what needs to happen. I say more power to him!"

The young man's face reddened. He took off his thick gloves and safety glasses and stormed toward the break room. There sat Charlie and his maintenance team having coffee and talking about anything and everything other than fixing the afflicted machine.

"What's that mean?" the young man demanded.

"What's *what* mean?" Charlie asked with a warm smile, his thick Alabama dialect drawling extra syllables into each word.

"What's it mean that you can fix a problem with a cup of coffee?"

"Well," drawled Charlie as he cooled his coffee by blowing across its surface, "when you've studied a problem from every conceivable angle and can't seem to find a solution, sometimes the best you can do is walk away from it completely. Then, when you come back with clear, fresh eyes, you see the answer."

The young man stood, with mouth agape.

Charlie toasted him with his cup. "You see, son, the answer is right there in front of us, we're just looking too hard for it. As soon as we back off a little, we'll see it."

And they did. Ten minutes later, Charlie's crew reassembled around the machine, and the answer seemed to leap out at them. It was repaired, and the mill was up and running again.

Charlie is now retired as head of maintenance for the steel mill. He's free to pursue his two greatest passions: flying and teaching others to fly.

"Every person learns differently," Charlie says. "After teaching hundreds of people to fly, I've learned that I have to approach each part of the training differently based on the strengths and limitations of the student. And, yep, sometimes that means stepping away from training and having a cup of coffee to give myself time to detach so that I can figure out what's best for that particular student."

As with every other person presented in this series, Charlie agrees that happiness is a choice. Happiness is something to be cultivated and exercised. Then, like a muscle, it becomes stronger and more and more a part of who we are.

"There are so many lessons we can learn about life from being a pilot," Charlie says. "Flying a plane is a great metaphor for happiness." He provides three happiness lessons using this metaphor.

1. **It takes resistance to fly:** Lift, which is the force that allows an airplane to become airborne, is caused by the resistance of the air against the wing. The propeller pulls the plane forward, but it's the air striking the wing that allows the plane to fly.

    "People seem to feel like something's wrong if life is resisting them," says Charlie. "That's not the case at all. If you're moving forward, you're going to encounter resistance, and it's that resistance that lets you fly. You've got to expect resistance; it's showing you that you're making progress."

    Let's say you want to try or do something new. When you first try it, you'll discover that it's more difficult than you thought. "Well," explains Charlie, "that can be a reason to quit or an indication that you need to work harder and get better. Either one is okay, but it's your choice."

    Charlie continues, "Resistance helps you find out what you're made of so that you can improve and move forward."

    The same is true for what you believe. If other people resist your point of view on something, it's a chance to check in with yourself and see if you truly believe what you are saying and to clarify and change or, ideally, strengthen your perspective.

2. **Take two deep breaths:** There is a series of steps to becoming a full pilot. The first one is to become certified as a VFR (Visual Flight Rules) aviator. This means that you can only fly on clear days and away from clouds.

However, regardless of how closely you monitor sky conditions, at some point most new pilots accidentally fly into a cloud. This is extremely dangerous because you become disoriented and can no longer tell the direction you are heading or whether you're ascending or descending. It's quite common to develop vertigo in these situations, which can lead to panic and tragic circumstances.

When VFR pilots fly into a cloud, their first reaction is typically to try and get out as quickly as possible, but this is the worst thing they can do.

Just as Charlie found that a cup of coffee can fix most things, he recommends that a pilot caught in a cloud take two slow, deep breaths before doing *anything*. "This gives you a chance to relax and calm down. Then, you can *act* calmly rather than *react* in panic.

"When we run into a problem in life," Charlie continues, "people tend to jump to a solution rather than give themselves a little time to get their bearings and then make a good choice. Whether you're in a plane or soaring through life, when you go into a cloud, take two slow breaths before you do anything."

3. **Aviate, navigate, communicate:** Charlie says, "When there's a problem during flight, most new pilots want to grab the microphone and tell the controllers on the ground." At this Charlie begins to laugh, "What's the guy on the ground going to do when you're five thousand feet up in the sky?

"No," continues Charlie, "the first thing is to aviate. That is—fly the plane. Make sure your altitude is high and safe enough. Then navigate—make sure you're on course. Lastly, and only after you've done the other two, communicate with anyone who might need to know."

When things go wrong in life, we first need to aviate—raise the altitude of our attitude as high as possible. We need to summon our courage, our faith, and our gratitude so that we are internally as high as we can be in that moment.

Next, we need to navigate—choose a course. If we choose a course when we're upset, there's a very good chance we'll choose the wrong direction.

Lastly, we need to communicate. When things go wrong, many people communicate, communicate, and communicate with anyone and everyone, spreading and magnifying their problem with each person they talk to. Tell other people about your situation only after you have reached your highest internal altitude and selected a course to follow. Then they can support you along your journey.

Make a decision to be happy even when you experience resistance, take two breaths when you fly into a cloud of problems, and remember that you should always aviate (set your altitude) first, navigate (choose your course) second, and then, and only then, communicate with others.

And if all else fails, go have a cup of coffee.

FORGIVENESS—
A PATHWAY TO
HAPPINESS

After the man she loves betrays her, a woman finds the pathway to happiness through forgiveness.

Forgiveness does not change the past, but it does enlarge the future.
—Paul Boese

ou what?" Susan asked in disbelief.

Jack didn't respond. He sat slumped in a kitchen chair, his massive shoulders stooped and trembling. Tears rolled down his round red cheeks—cheeks that were more typically pressed back into a large and engaging smile. He stared at the floor, whispering incoherently.

"Did you just say that you quit your job?" Susan asked not sure she had heard correctly.

For a long moment the only sound was the clack-clack-clack of the lawn sprinkler outside the open window and the soft sobs coming from her beloved husband.

Jack nodded silently, and Susan felt as if life had drained from her body. The bag of groceries that rested on her hip now felt as if it weighed a hundred pounds. She let it slide down to the counter, where it landed with a thud and then toppled over. Blueberries spread out across the counter surface and spilled onto the floor.

Dozens of thoughts and questions flashed in Susan's mind. First came thoughts of practicality: *What about our health insurance? He's a diabetic and recently had open-heart surgery. Will we lose our house? How will we pay for his son's college? We don't have enough money saved up to retire.*

Then came questions and thoughts Susan wasn't proud of: *He's too old to begin a new career. Will I have to give up my writing and go back to work? What will my friends think?*

Susan slid into the chair next to Jack, inhaled deeply, and grasped his big paw in her hands. She squeezed tightly and said, "It's okay. We'll get through this. I love you."

Jack looked into Susan's eyes. He was a big, powerful man—not only physically powerful, but as a successful bank vice president, he was powerful in their community as well. Hunched over as he was, he looked deflated and powerless like a frightened child.

As if suddenly awakened from a dream, Susan asked, "But what happened?"

"Someone in my department is stealing," Jack said.

"But why would *you* quit?" Susan asked.

"I'm the guy in charge," he said. "They needed someone to blame, and they put it on me. It was either resign or be fired."

"We'll get through this," she repeated. "Together, we'll get through this."

Susan reminded herself that it was Jack she loved and not the stuff his job provided. After an abusive and painful first marriage and then raising her daughter alone for ten years, Susan thought she would never find someone she could love and trust until she met Jack. Their life had been—and would continue to be—wonderful because they had each other, and that's what was important.

Then came the phone call.

"Susan Hoskins? I'm Special Agent Morganfield with the FBI," the caller said in a husky voice. "I'm not supposed to be speaking to you, and if anyone asks I'll deny our conversation."

Susan felt like she had stepped into a bad espionage movie. The voice continued, "The thief at your husband's bank . . . well, the thief *is* your husband. We've been building a case against him for more than a year now. As the head of the commercial real estate department, Jack was accepting checks from purchasers and then depositing them into his own account."

Susan's mind collapsed in on itself.

"Are you there?" the caller asked.

Susan nodded her head, forgetting that the person on the other end of the phone line couldn't see her silent answer to his question.

Feeling anger and resentment percolate through her body, Susan spat, "I don't believe it . . . *you're lying!*" And then she demanded, "*Who is this?*"

"Susan," the voice said compassionately, "I'm Special Agent Morganfield with the FBI. I'm violating our code of ethics speaking to you, but you need to know that your husband is going to be charged with dozens of counts of theft and fraud. You need to get away, and you need to get a lawyer."

"Why do *I* need a lawyer?" Susan asked plaintively.

"Because the prosecutors and civil attorneys will try and show that you were complicit in his actions. But from everything I've seen, you weren't involved."

A second's silence stretched into infinity.

"I have to go," the caller said. "Good luck, Susan. Please take my advice. Bad things are coming."

And they came.

The man she loved, the man she trusted, the man with whom she shared her most intimate secrets, as well as her bed, turned out to be an embezzler—and not a very smart one. He was depositing the stolen money into his personal account at the very bank he was stealing from.

Their home was seized as well as their cars, bank accounts, retirement funds, and all other assets. Stories splashed across the front pages of the local paper and evening news with pictures of Jack being led off to jail in handcuffs. Previously she had wondered how she would take her friends' and family's judgment over Jack being a middle-aged, unemployed banker. Now she was experiencing their reactions to his being a thief.

Susan was ostracized. She didn't know which stung more fiercely—the looks of pity or the looks of contempt.

She took solace in the fact that things couldn't get worse.

But then they did.

Looking through Jack's papers while he sat in jail awaiting trial, Susan came upon more startling revelations. Jack had lied to her about his military service and even his college history.

Susan's heart turned to ice when she discovered that another story Jack had told her was a fabrication. He had completely made up having had twins from a prior marriage who died as infants.

Jack had been lying to her for more than a decade, and she had been blind to it all. The man she knew and loved turned out to be pure fiction. She lay in bed at night seething with anger not only at him, but also at herself for having been so gullible—so stupid!

That was seventeen years ago. Today, Susan is married to a man she adores and who adores her. She has written five books and continues pursuing her passions: writing, photography, and yoga.

More importantly, she is happy. When I interviewed Susan, she freely admitted that she was happy, but it was an admission that didn't need to be made. Susan exudes happiness. To be around her is to feel the joy and tranquility of someone who has been through hell and has come out on the other side stronger and happier. She is happiness personified.

"The key is forgiveness," she says. "Not just forgiveness for Jack, but forgiveness for myself, because whenever someone hurts us or takes advantage of us there is a part of us that blames ourselves as being deserving of such treatment. I had to let all of that go." Susan offers her three suggestions for becoming happier.

1. **Forgiveness is a process:** According to Susan, you don't just forgive and have all the pain, hurt, and negative energy melt away. It takes time and intentional effort. You have to repeatedly let go of your resentment for what has transpired, and this takes time.

    To that end, we have to be patient and gentle with ourselves, and we do this through forgiveness. Susan says, "I knew that the process of forgiveness was complete when I could appreciate the woman I had become as a result of this experience. During this challenging time, people often asked me how I was able to keep a positive attitude. The choice was simple. I could either succumb to bitterness or rise above victimhood and celebrate life. I chose life with all of its betrayals and disappointments. Forgiveness of self and others is a choice to celebrate life."

2. **Forgiveness through reflection:** Susan says, "Forgiveness for Jack came with the understanding that what we see and judge in another person is really a reflection of ourselves. Therefore, I had to explore where I had fallen short in being honest with myself and other people."

3. **Forgiveness through resilience:** "Forgiveness for myself came through the process of discovering that I could be and do more than I ever thought possible," Susan explains. "I had a choice either to succumb to the despair of losing everything, or rise to the incredible challenge of proving that I in no way participated in, or benefited from, Jack's criminal behavior."

It's been said that nothing makes you dance like having your feet in the fire. Susan went through the fire of disappointment, loss, and betrayal, and learned that through the process of forgiveness she could dance with genuine happiness.

HAPPY ON PURPOSE

A medical doctor from the United States forgoes the money and prestige of private practice to find happiness by living his life's purpose building hospitals in Africa.

Your purpose in life is to find your purpose and give your whole heart and soul to it.
—the Buddha

H e's five feet one, but you'd never think of him as short. He's eighty-five, but it would never occur to you to describe him as old.

He walks with a cane, but you'd never label him as frail.

He's eighteen years past the average retirement age in the United States, yet he shows no signs of slowing down. In fact, he's revving up!

"Retirement?" Dr. Dennis Lofstrom scoffed when I mentioned the word. "I'm not into retirement," he said. "I'm into re-*fire*-ment!"

When I asked Dr. Lofstrom ("Dr. Denny" to his friends) if he considers himself to be a happy person, he answered with a confident and resolute, "Absolutely!"

Happy people believe they are happy. This is one of the secrets to happiness. No one who believes him or herself to be unhappy is actually happy. Happiness is a mind-set, and as all of the people who will share their happy stories with us in this series agree, happiness is an inside job.

When you first meet Dr. Denny, it's his enormous clear-blue eyes and broad smile that catch your attention and, more than that, draw you in. He exudes warmth and compassion, and his offset grin seems to say that he knows the punch line to some great cosmic joke.

He's the biological father to eleven children and the honorary father to hundreds.

"I've always wanted to help people," he told me. "I can remember when I was thirteen, going to a youth conference in Moline, Illinois, being held at a Lutheran seminary. As part of the program, American doctors who had chosen to serve in Africa were invited to share their experiences."

He talks of this event seventy-two–and-a-half years ago as if it were last night.

"They were so happy, you know? I could see it in their eyes. These doctors were happy, and I wanted to be happy like them," he said eagerly.

He was barely a teenager, and he knew not only his life's purpose, but that following this purpose would bring him happiness.

I had dinner with Dr. Denny and his wife-nurse-partner, Paula, not too long ago. "There are eighteen million children under the age of fourteen living in Tanzania," he said, grabbing a paper napkin and a pen. "And there isn't a single children's hospital in the whole country . . . but there will be, soon!"

For the next several minutes, they excitedly sketched their plans for a 41.5-acre children's hospital near Dar es Salaam, Tanzania. Building hospitals in Africa is no pipe dream for Dr. Denny and Paula.

International Health Partners TZ, the nonprofit agency they helped found, has a proud history of building medical facilities in Tanzania. After rehabilitating Iambi Hospital in central Tanzania, they went on to develop the St. John's University School of Nursing at Dodoma—the largest nursing school in Tanzania. They next built the Nyakato Health Center in Mwanza.

"Having something new and exciting to look forward to is one of the keys to happiness, and having a purpose that is constantly pulling you forward assures new and exciting discoveries every day," said Dr. Denny.

"But what about people who don't know their purpose?" I asked.

"What do you mean?" Dr. Denny asked, his eyes narrowing but his smile unwavering.

"Well," I said, "not everyone figures out at the age of thirteen what they want to do with their lives. In fact, it seems that most people go their entire lives uncertain as to whether they are on the right track."

"Discovering your purpose is a lot easier than you think," he said. "Just pay attention to three things."

1. **Nuances:** Notice the gentle prodding in your mind and heart that tells you that you would enjoy going in a certain direction. Believe that you have a purpose, and then listen to your intuition; it will guide you toward what you are meant

to do—what will give you the greatest satisfaction and the highest levels of happiness.

2. **Coincidences:** Notice the roads that end, inviting you to change course or backtrack and consider another route. And pay attention to the roads that open up before you that you might not have considered in the past.

    Dr. Denny says, "I believe being chosen to be part of the youth delegation to that conference back in 1931 was a coincidence that was *no* coincidence; it was designed to help me find my purpose. Coincidences are there to reveal our path to us."

3. **Cosmic two-by-fours:** You can take a step one day in a direction that is not best suited to your purpose. Then the next day you take another step along this path, and then another. Soon you have walked away from what would most bring you happiness and satisfaction. It is then that, to quote Dr. Denny, "The universe whacks you across the back of the head with a cosmic two-by-four."

    "For me, that happened in 2001," said Dr. Denny. "We were back in the United States and planned to stay here, but the terrorist strike of 9/11 caused our investments to crash. With debts to pay, we liquidated our stocks at 75 percent below what they had been worth just a few months before— we were broke. It was at that time that a dear friend called and asked us to come and help out for 'just ten weeks' in Tanzania. We've now been there for more than a decade.

    "The cosmic two-by-four hurts, sure," he says. "But it's the only thing strong enough to wake you up and make you realize that you're headed in the wrong direction."

So how is Dr. Denny spending what many would term his golden years?

"I spend two-thirds of my time in Tanzania working on the hospital, and the other third of the year traveling across the United States, trying to drum up donations and volunteers to make it a reality."

When I tracked down Dr. Denny to interview him via Skype, he and Paula were in a small motel just outside of Albuquerque, New Mexico.

"Twenty-seven dollars a night!" boomed Paula with unbridled excitement.

"I beg your pardon," I said.

"The motel," she explained. "It's only twenty-seven dollars a night. Isn't that great?"

I imagined a lackluster twenty-seven-dollar-a-night motel as I said, "Oh, yes, that's wonderful."

Sensing my bemusement, Paula explained, "Okay, yes! That's a really cheap motel in the United States. But that's a month's salary for a worker in Tanzania. The more frugal we are here, the more we can do there."

As she spoke, Denny's head nodded in agreement.

When we concluded, I thought, *Wow, could they really be that happy to find a cheap motel room?*

And then I realized: No, Dr. Denny and Paula are happy because they are living their purpose. They have a sense of mission—a genuine connection with life and with others. They are giving of themselves every day, and they are truly happy on purpose!

HAPPY TO BE OF SERVICE

International Health Partners TZ: www.ihptz.org

HAPPINESS IN A HUG

A small woman makes a big impact on people's happiness.

*Millions and millions of years would still not give me half
enough time to describe that tiny instant of all eternity when
you put your arms around me and I put my arms around you.*
—Jacques Prévert

C arol stared at the official-looking form for several
minutes.

Organization name?

Okay, got that, she thought.

Contact person?

Carol had written in her full legal name.

Carol scanned back through the document to see if she had
forgotten anything. She hadn't.

The form was complete, except for one empty line. The information requested vexed Carol. Finally, she wrote her most honest
response on the line and returned the form to the stern-looking
official who had given it to her.

The man peered down through the reading glasses perched on the tip of his nose.

When he got to Carol's answer to the vexing question, the official read what she had written. He then gazed up at Carol as if trying to figure her out.

Carol aimed an unwavering, authentic smile at the man.

"Um . . . okay," he said, peering back down at the form. "Your name is Ms. Miller, right?"

"Carol Miller," she replied.

"Yeah . . . uh-huh . . . Carol Miller," the man said, clearing his voice and sitting a little straighter. "And you want to protest giving people hugs." The man's left eyebrow arched inquisitively.

"No," she answered.

The man leaned forward over his desk. "It says right here that you want to protest giving people hugs."

"I know," she said. "But we don't want to protest *against* hugging people, we want to hug people."

"Then why did you fill out a form asking to hold a public protest?" the man asked, raising his voice two octaves higher.

"Because you don't have a form to allow people to stand around and offer hugs to perfect strangers," Carol replied, her voice laden with sunshine. "When I talked to the management office at the Navy Pier and asked if I and some other people could stand outside with a sign that said Free Hugs, they said they couldn't allow us to do that, but they could allow us to protest, if that's what we wanted."

The man's face was expressionless as Carol continued: "We wanted to do things the right way—so, if filling out a form for a protest is what's required to allow us to offer people hugs, then I'll fill out the form."

The man's expression seemed to say, *Lady, you're crazy,* but his demeanor remained cordial and official. Reaching for the rubber stamp that lay between them, the man tapped the stamp on the ink pad two quick times, and then slammed it down on Carol's form with a *thunk!*

"Happy protesting," he said, sliding the form back to Carol.

"We're approved?" Carol asked.

"Yeah . . . you're approved," the man said as he turned his attention to the next person.

"Great!" Carol squealed, grabbing the form and turning around to leave. Then she spun around to face him once more.

"Can I give *you* a hug?" she asked him.

"Uh . . . no," he replied. "I'm . . . uh . . . I'm good."

With a whatever-makes-you-happy shrug, Carol turned and bounced toward the door.

Carol had heard about a man in Australia who frequented busy places offering hugs to passersby. She thought it would be a good idea to do the same thing in her native Chicago. Carol enlisted hugging volunteers and selected the Navy Pier because of the wide variety of people who frequent this large and bustling tourist destination.

"I was smart to select such a high-traffic location," Carol said with pride. "Unfortunately, I didn't do so well when selecting the date."

With a self-deprecating laugh, Carol said, "Outdoors in mid-January on the lake in Chicago is neither the time nor the place for foot traffic."

Six volunteers showed up that wintery day. For two hours they bounced in place and hugged one another to stay warm.

"We didn't get many people receiving hugs that day," said Carol. That was in 2008, and the meager response didn't dampen

Carol's enthusiasm. In fact, a couple of years ago, she set an intention to go global.

Carol e-mailed friends and family members, asking them to invite people in all fifty states as well as in every country of the world to join in on the selected day to give free hugs.

"It's amazing what you see when we do one of these events," Carol said. "People will run across the street when they see the signs just to get a hug. Other people, typically older people, will say that our hug was the first human contact they had received in weeks."

Carol wants the world to experience the power of hugs. And she's not shy about soliciting support for her cause. After reaching out to dozens of world and religious leaders, Carol was gratified to find out that at least one of them was on board. The assistant to Bishop Desmond Tutu—the South African–born antiapartheid activist and winner of the Nobel Peace Prize—informed Carol that he would hang a Free Hugs sign next to him while on a speaking tour of Florida.

Carol, who is only four foot ten, accomplishes big things for a small person. People who meet her wonder how so much happiness can be packed into such a little container. Carol is a person who shines with happiness. To become as happy as Carol, consider her three suggestions.

1. **Don't jump to conclusions:** We tend to react, or more often overreact, before we fully understand what's happening, and our reactions can upset people around us, creating messes that we have to clean up. Cleaning up messy relationship issues detracts from happiness, so think before you speak.

    And then if you still can't speak nicely, think some more.

2. **Be gentle with yourself:** "We tend to beat ourselves up," Carol explains. "So much of our focus is negative, and that leads to negative feelings about ourselves.

   "When you take a test and get 94 out of 100 correct, the teacher typically writes a big red minus 6 on the page. Rather than celebrating the 94 correct, the focus is on the 6 you got wrong. We do this to ourselves, focusing on our shortcomings rather than on our strengths."

3. **Look for things to be grateful for:** "Even in your biggest struggles, there is something to be grateful for," Carol reminds us. "Every day there are things to be grateful for. You may be struggling to pay your mortgage, but you've got a bed to sleep in."

   If all else fails, give someone a hug. Hugging boosts the neuropeptide oxytocin, which has a lowering effect on blood pressure, promotes well-being, and even improves memory.

THE GREAT
HAPPINESS
EXPERIMENT

**A woman and her husband conduct an
experiment with their own lives to discover
what really makes them happy.**

The unexamined life is not worth living.
—Socrates

H old still," Kate teased as she grabbed the crown of
Paul's head with her left hand. Steadying the razor in
her right, Kate continued to shave Paul's scalp.

As she turned to rinse the razor, Paul grabbed Kate around
the waist and pulled her playfully onto his lap. Holding the razor
high for safety, Kate threw her arms around Paul and hugged
him tightly, getting shaving cream in her eye in the process.

As Kate leaned back to reach for a towel, Paul gently grabbed
her cheeks and pulled her gaze to his. With a playful smile, he
asked, "Are you sure about this?"

Paul and Kate Lindholm were about to engage in a jointly designed experiment, delving into the very depths of what makes people happy. They were to be the guinea pigs. This experiment would entail studying and documenting every aspect of their lives.

Looking at the swath of freshly shaved skin atop Paul's head, Kate drew in a deep breath.

"Well? Are you sure you want to do this?" Paul asked again.

Kate smiled resolutely and chirped, "Yes!" She pulled Paul's partially shaved head forward and planted a big kiss on top to seal the deal. Kate noticed how smooth Paul's scalp felt on her lips and then glanced over his shoulder to see her own reflection in the mirror.

I'm next, Kate thought, trying to imagine herself without hair.

Kate and Paul had already begun to wear what they called "the uniform." Every day the couple dressed in matching clothes consisting of coastal-blue work pants, a blue shirt, and nondescript shoes. Each carried what they called "the box"—a plastic toolbox that replaced a purse or wallet. Either Paul or Kate carried a small camera in the box at all times to document their experiment.

"With a background in science, I know that scientific experimentation can help you isolate causal factors—often called the X variable, and we wanted to figure out what the X variable for happiness is, for us, at least," Kate said. "We eliminated a lot of extraneous things from our lives and then recorded our feelings, behavior, and expressions."

Kate smiled as she shook her head. "We were surprised to find out that the things that made us happier were actually the things we thought were set up just for the experiment."

These are three of the things Kate and Paul discovered that lead to increased happiness.

1. **Simplify your life:** Kate explains, "People seem to think that having lots of choices for everything is best. We found the opposite to be true. As we eliminated a lot of things from our lives so that we could notice what increased our happiness, we found that we became more content because we had fewer decisions to make.

   "When you go to the store to buy deodorant, there are dozens of brands, and you're never quite sure if you bought the best one for you. Even if you have a favorite brand, manufacturers are always trying to get you to switch by offering incentives. So now you have a new decision to make—stay with the trusted brand or try something new that may not work as well. This is stressful, and we face thousands of little decisions like this every day."

   By living more simply, cutting down on things, and narrowing their range of choices, Paul and Kate discovered that they felt less anxious.

   "If you've got twenty pairs of shoes, your choice as to what pair to wear is multiplied by 2,000 percent. Making decisions is stressful, and stress leads to being less happy. In addition, that's twenty pairs of shoes that need to be shined and stored.

   "You don't have to shave your head to eliminate deciding how you will style your hair, like we did. But look at things that you can diminish, release, and eliminate. Pare down your life. Not only is more not better, but the stress of having more can also make you less happy."

2. **Make meal planning a celebration:** This suggestion is actually an extension of the first. Kate says, "Do you realize how

much time and attention we give to eating and yet how poorly most people eat? We, especially we women, are always thinking about what we are going to prepare for the next meal."

Kate realized that she, like most people, stresses over the questions below more than twenty times a week:

- Do I have the necessary ingredients?
- Do I have time to cook and clean up?
- Will the other person like what I've prepared?
- Is what we're going to eat healthy?

She and Paul discovered that shopping and preparing all of their meals at one time for the week made them both happier and healthier.

"On Sundays, Paul and I would go to the store and buy everything we would eat for that week. We would then go home, turn on some music, open some wine, chop vegetables, and cook together. It was actually pretty romantic."

Kate and Paul would then refrigerate portioned meals that they could microwave in about a minute. "Think about it," says Kate, "rather than struggling with what to prepare— cooking and cleaning nearly two dozen times every week— we did it once. So not only did we save all the work involved in meal preparation and cleanup, we also eliminated the stress of decision making—and that's what really made us feel happier. Plus, rather than trying to throw a meal together at the end of the day when we were tired and hope that it was both healthy and tasty, we'd already made those decisions."

3. **Rest is more important than work:** Most people go to work in the morning and do their job for eight or nine hours a day, five to six days a week. However, with the advent of

technology, many people never quite stop working, and this can make them less happy and, surprisingly, *less* effective.

Kate says, "Paul and I tried to figure out if there was a perfect ratio for work and rest. First, we both worked eight-hour days, and then we tried splitting the day up differently. We would work four hours on, four hours off, and then four hours on. We made note of how happy we felt working this way. Next, we worked two hours on, two off, two on, two off, etc. And we documented how we felt. What we discovered was that it doesn't matter so much the schedule, so long as there are frequent opportunities to rest.

"And we don't just mean naps. Rest means letting your work go completely and engaging in other things that are important to you. Because of cell phones that allow for texting, e-mails, and even document creation and editing, the line between work and play is getting blurred, and people are not fully stopping work to rest and play. They don't get the downtime that makes them feel rejuvenated and makes them more creative."

Many people live under the misconception that if they work constantly, they will one day be caught up and then be able to relax, but work always compounds, bringing more to do. "To be happy," Kate says, "build your life around your free time and fit your work in, rather than the other way around. You'll be happier and more productive as a result."

Kate and Paul no longer wear the uniform, shave their heads, or carry the box. However, they have kept their life simple and enjoy preparing meals together. And they create their schedules with an eye toward what will make them happy first, and then what will make them money.

"Most people never even stop to think about happiness or what brings them happiness," Kate says with a grin. "For us, making happiness our highest priority has made us mindful of being happy. It is that mindfulness that has led to our feeling happier."

ALIVE WITH HAPPINESS

A man near death finds happiness in his passion for life.

When you arise in the morning, give thanks for the food and for the joy of living. If you see no reason for giving thanks, the fault lies only in yourself.
—Tecumseh

Robert heard the sound.

It wasn't a loud sound.

Nearly everyone has heard it, but few have heard it up close. For many, it's the last sound they will ever hear, and Robert Shan, age forty-one, presumed the sound was the overture for his death.

Robert had just arrived home to his native Jamaica. As soon as the plane from Nassau landed, Robert called his mother.

"She's my heartbeat," he said. "I love my mother. She has made me who I am."

As Robert stepped from the phone booth, he was approached by a police officer asking to see his ID. Robert fished in his pocket for his passport, but then he got the unsettling feeling that the man who stood before him wasn't really interested in his identification. The man seemed to be sizing Robert up in a way that made Robert take an unconscious half step back.

While taking a cursory glance at Robert's passport, the man pulled a blue steel handgun from his jacket and jabbed it into Robert's stomach.

Robert slumped and emitted a low *oof*.

While Robert was doubled over, rubbing his abdomen, he could see the ragged shoes of another man approaching. Hunched over as he was, Robert could see his assailant's feet as well. The man holding the gun wore threadbare tennis shoes.

The pieces clicked into place, and Robert realized that this man was not a police officer as he'd claimed, but a thief.

"Grab his stuff, and let's get the hell out of here," the second man said, spitting his words out at a fearful staccato pace.

The two men jumped Robert. First, they stripped him of his watch and bracelet, scratching his wrists in the process. Next, they wrenched the rings from his fingers and tore his wallet from his pants pocket.

"Let's go!" shouted the second man, shoving some of Robert's belongings into his jacket while taking a few hurried steps away.

"Lie down," commanded the first man as he violently poked Robert's gut once more with the point of the gun.

"Are you crazy?" his partner stammered. "We just got out! You do this and they'll catch us for sure. Do you wanna go back to prison?"

"Lie down!" the first man barked.

Robert dropped slowly to his hands and knees.

"I said *lie* down!" his attacker screamed, kicking Robert forcefully from behind. Robert crumbled forward into a bush.

The man stood on the back of Robert's neck. Robert's face began to bleed from being pricked by a tangle of thorny leaves.

Robert felt the gun barrel being pressed into the back of his head. It was then that he heard the unmistakable sound, the sound of the gun's hammer being cocked.

"You're going to die tonight," the assailant hissed.

"C'mon, man!" his compatriot whined, shifting nervously from foot to foot.

"Hey! Did you hear me, fat boy?" the man asked, pressing the barrel harder into Robert's skull and repeating each syllable precisely for emphasis, "You-are-go-ing-to-die-to-night."

Robert squeezed his eyes tight and braced his body, awaiting his inevitable fate.

"In that moment, I gave up," Robert said two years later. "Death was an absolute certainty. I was going to die, and that would be the end of it. I just let go of my attachment to life because, for me, life was over."

That night, a twist of fate saved Robert.

At the very moment Robert lay prostrate in the sticker bush and yielded to death, another hapless man came upon the scene. Walking alone and seeming to be a little tipsy, the man's smart clothing and twinkling jewelry was like blood in the water for two sharks.

Having seized Robert's meager possessions, the two predators were distracted by a bigger fish.

When Robert was certain that the men were no longer focused on him, he leapt to his feet and made a break for it. Tears streaming down his face, Robert ran until his legs burned and his chest ached.

"I woke up early the next morning, and for the first time in my life I realized how lucky—how incredibly lucky—I was just to be alive," Robert said.

Through his perpetual smile, Robert continued, "I've never lost that feeling."

Robert gazed appreciatively out of the window as if he were drinking in the beauty of a masterful work of art. He sighed a long, contented sigh. "Everything is just so beautiful when you realize how lucky you are to be alive. For me, that's being able to see the palm trees flowing in the breeze, to hear the sound of children laughing, to taste a fresh mango. Life is delicious.

"I am truly happy," Robert said, grateful for the gift of happiness.

Today, Robert works as a waiter at the Sandals Resort in Montego Bay, Jamaica. After only four months as an employee there, Robert received the Employee of the Year Award because of his effusive happiness and joyful service.

Robert offers three tips for happiness.

1. **Be grateful just to be alive:** "If you knew—really knew—that at any moment your life would end, you would be filled with peace and unattached to the problems and difficulties of living."

   Life is the most precious thing we all possess, and it is probably taken for granted the most. If you, like Robert, truly believed you were about to die, you would see life for the gift that it is.

   Robert advises us to be mindful of every day, as one day will be our last.

2. **Build a better reflection:** Robert's apple-shaped cheeks swell when he smiles. His beaming grin is received by others and mirrored back to him.

"I love to make other people smile," Robert said. "If you come into my restaurant and you're having a bad day, I get to help make you smile. That's my greatest joy—helping other people feel happy.

"We both win," Robert continued, "I then get to be around happy people." Robert's smile bent into a playful smirk. "And that makes me happy."

3. **Live *irie*:** Whenever two Jamaicans meet, they typically exchange the greeting "*Wa gwan?*" which is slang for "What's going on?"

"Me, I'm *irie*" is the common response.

In Jamaican patois, the word *irie* means "good." It also means "happy."

In the lilting, sun-drenched tones of a Jamaican native, Robert explained: "When people ask you '*Wa gwan?*' all day, and you respond, 'me, I'm happy,' it reminds you to be happy.

"Maybe this is why we Jamaicans have such a reputation for being happy," Robert said with a laugh.

Without exception, happy people believe they are happy. When someone asks, "How are you?" remind yourself of the truth and respond: "I'm happy."

FROM FEAR TO HAPPINESS

A woman and her husband leave a homeland torn by civil war and find happiness waiting in their new country.

The fear of death is more to be dreaded than death itself.
—Publilius Syrus

Sumithra Lokugamage sat at her desk, head down, engrossed in her work. Sunlight poured through the large office windows, and the smell of morning tea filled the air. The morning had been busy, but not atypically so. Sumithra focused on completing her current project against another tight deadline.

A distant *foom!* caused her to slowly raise her head. "Not again," she said in a helpless whisper.

Sumithra's colleagues ran past her to the windows.

"Do you see it?" one asked.

"Over there!" cried another.

Everyone's hands became busy. Some covered their mouths in shock. Others clutched their chests as if trying to stop a breaking heart. Still others grabbed stationary objects to steady their wobbling legs. Most reached for cell phones and pressed buttons frantically.

Sumithra could see an enormous plume of gray smoke spreading rapidly up and over a distant building.

"That's the school!" a woman shrieked. "That's my child's school!"

"No," a nervous man said from over her shoulder. "That's not the school. That's a . . . that's a government building!"

It had been six months. Six months without an explosion. Now, as Sumithra and the people she worked with stared out the window, they all wondered the same thing, *Are my loved ones safe?*

This was Colombo, Sri Lanka, in 1998. At the time, life there was consumed by hauntingly sporadic bombings, endless rumors of future bombings, and the frustration and dehumanization of endless security checkpoints.

The Sri Lankan civil war began in 1983 when a group of militant separatists sought to seize power. As tends to happen in such David and Goliath conflicts where the government is the giant, a common ploy used by insurgents is to strike terror into the hearts of the people with the intent of crumbling support for that government.

"A high political official would be executed and there would be a funeral," Sumithra said. "It was a near certainty that a suicide bomber would be at the funeral attempting to kill as many innocent people as possible."

Sumithra continued, her voice lilting with that friendly and inviting accent Americans tend to ascribe only to people from

India, "We were always in fear. When you are constantly afraid, your humanity leaves you. You don't feel anything—you don't respect people. The value of humans—that thing, well, that thing is not there."

Sumithra and her husband, Prasad, moved to the United States, where after a decade and a half they have shed most of the fear that coated them like a film for so many years.

"We didn't realize how much we were afraid until we moved to the safety of the United States. Many people have no idea what it's really like," Sumithra says, choking back her emotions. "You could be standing next to someone—someone just like anybody you know, and then that person detonates a bomb not only killing himself but also hoping that you will die, too.

"When that is your life *each and every day*, you shift. You shut down. You no longer care for people. You live in constant fear. And it is impossible to be afraid and happy at the same time."

With so much violence all around for so many years, people get immune to it and become less human. As Sumithra described, "a bomb here, a bomb there—people get killed and you get used to it."

The first casualty of any war is happiness. The purpose of war is to bring as much despair and unhappiness to the other side as possible. When there is enough unhappiness, the citizens will support the ceding of part or all of the power. When the government, regardless of its power, loses the support of enough people, it is doomed.

"In Sri Lanka, there was a very good chance that you or someone you loved could be killed at any time," Sumithra said. "We lived in survival mode. Happiness is not even something you consider when you are incapable of trusting anyone and your life could end at any second."

Sumithra didn't even know what happiness was until she came to the United States.

And now, after living in America for more than a decade and a half, she can finally say: "Here, now, I have room in my life for happiness, and I feel it all the time."

Happiness is a new way of living for Sumithra, and she works to expand her happiness. Here are three things Sumithra suggests we remember to become happier.

1. **You can't be happy when you are afraid:** If you face fear and do what frightens you, you will free yourself of fear. So many people go through life feeling mildly to moderately afraid of certain people, circumstances, and activities. This fear diminishes their happiness.

    Facing the potential pain of embarrassment or rejection and taking a risk to face what you are afraid of liberates you from fear and opens you up to feel happier.

2. **You can't be happy when you are angry:** Anger—especially anger in situations that are relatively insignificant—is often a learned trait taught to us as children by our parents.

    Anger raises our blood pressure and creates fear and frustration for people around us. In addition, our emotions vibrate with the shocks and aftershocks of our anger. As a result, we feel less happy.

    Becoming slow to anger and, better yet, learning to rarely become angry is a powerful skill to develop along the road to happiness. Overcoming anger begins with a decision that you will master your anger, and then try as best as you can to hold your temper each and every time something upsets you.

    Sumithra says, "I have tried not to become angry. I have done it for a long time, and I'm pretty good at it."

3. **You can't be happy when you are complaining:** Complaining amplifies problems, it doesn't diminish them. Complaining only increases being upset; it doesn't lessen it. If complaining made people feel better, then the biggest complainers would be the happiest people.

"If you call something a problem, it becomes a problem," Sumithra added.

After nearly two-thirds of life spent in fear of others, Sumithra offers one last suggestion for happiness: Try to see the good in people.

"Everyone who talks to me," she says, "I look for something good in them. When you do this, you learn something. You could learn something about life, you could learn something about other people. And," she says with a wise smile, "with any luck, you might just learn something about yourself."

THE LANGUAGE OF HAPPINESS

In Sinhala, a phonetic language spoken in Sri Lanka, the word for happiness is *sathuta* (sat-HU-tah).

TAKING A RISK FOR HAPPINESS

A man takes a risk and, as a result, discovers the route to success and happiness.

There are risks and costs to a program of action. But they are far less than the long-range risks and costs of comfortable inaction.
—John F. Kennedy

"This is ridiculous," Josh muttered under his breath.

He stretched his shoulders up to his ears and lowered them with a long, exasperated sigh. "The only thing more boring than a job where you sit around watching other people work," Josh said to no one except the inner windshield of his truck, "is a job where you sit around watching other people *not* work."

Quality control inspector. Josh Toye was twenty-nine years old and that was his title. He had applied for the lowest-wage job of unskilled laborer and was surprised to find out that the job was that of quality control inspector.

"You're basically a witness," the haggard foreman had rasped to Josh during his brief interview. "On every government construction job, there must be a quality control inspector. It's basically an employee who doesn't physically do the construction tasks but instead watches everything being done by the contractors and documents any discrepancies. That way, if there's a problem, we have someone who can report back as to what was and wasn't done."

Josh tried not to smile too broadly. He was struggling to take in what the man had just said. He would be paid for doing nothing. His "job" would be to sit and watch other people work.

This was Josh's dream job.

Or so he thought.

Josh discovered all too soon that sitting for long periods of time is boring—even if one is paid. He realized that he would much rather be one of the guys doing stuff than a guy watching stuff getting done.

On the third day of sitting and watching nothing, Josh ventured over to talk to one of the laborers.

"Why isn't anything happening?" Josh asked after exchanging pleasantries with the electrician's assistant.

"The government shut us down," the man reported without emotion. He, too, was being paid for doing nothing, but the arrangement appeared to suit him. He leaned back and took a long sip of his coffee drink.

"Again?" asked Josh.

The man nodded his head in slow resignation. "Yep, again."

"The government can assess a thousand-dollar-per-day penalty until we finish if we're not on time," Josh said.

The man gave Josh an explain-to-me-why-I-should-care look.

After talking to a couple of other workers, Josh found that a written schedule was all that was holding up their progress.

Josh's employer was installing sprinklers in the air traffic control tower at a major airport. In the understandable over-precaution that dictates security protocols for airports in post-9/11 America, the FAA simply could not allow workers carrying boxes of supplies and tools in and out of an active control tower without knowing precisely who would be doing what and when.

That night, Josh scoured the Internet for hours. He had watched the workers install the fire system, so he knew the make and model they were working with. Josh read everything he could find about the system.

Josh was about to risk his job by contradicting its prime directive: he was about to *do something*.

The following morning, Josh called the company that sold the fire system. The company sent a field rep out to the job site to give Josh a crash course on the system.

Next, Josh scheduled a meeting with his boss at the construction company, all of the contractors and subcontractors, and representatives of the FAA.

His job description could have read something like this . . .
Duties:

- Sit
- Observe
- Don't speak unless you're spoken to

. . . but Josh was taking responsibility for the successful completion of this project.

Josh got all the parties together so that collectively they could create a schedule that would ensure the work would be done on time, in the best possible way, and with minimal inconvenience to the controllers or their work.

The job was satisfactorily completed ahead of schedule.

Josh went from being the guy who watched things get done to the guy who made sure things got done. He became a project manager, ultimately handling more than $12 million in annual construction.

Today, Josh is on his own. As a successful contractor, home remodeler, and investor, he continues to take risks and figure out how to do things as he goes along.

"Nobody really knows how to do anything until they do it," Josh says. "But for some reason, people are afraid of being embarrassed, so they don't try new things.

"Today, with the Internet and people everywhere who are willing to advise you, you can figure out how to do just about anything," Josh reflected. "I didn't know how to install a hot-water heater until I installed three of them in one day."

If you ask Josh's friends, family, and clients who they feel is the happiest person they know, it would be a safe bet that nearly all would say Josh.

In a field dominated by looming deadlines and the stressful domino effect of dealing with subcontractors who have the proclivity of taking on more jobs than they can accomplish, Josh seems to glide through with a smile.

"I've worked at it," Josh explained. "Just like I'm always learning how to do new things on the job—whether it's sealing a deck or managing payroll and accounting—I'm always learning how to make myself happier, more productive, and a better dad."

Josh offers three suggestions for happiness.

1. **Clean up your environment:** "Whoever you are with rubs off on you," Josh said. "So, who are you hanging around with? That is, who is rubbing off on you?"

Seek out and hang out with people who enable you to feel happier and better about yourself, and who feel life is a happy adventure rather than a relentless drag.

2. **Take a risk:** The seeds of opportunity must always be planted in the field of uncertainty.

   Everything seems daunting until you give it a try. "Trying new things," Josh adds, "means always learning something new, which keeps you happy and looking forward to every day."

3. **Build your support team:** Josh has talked to and learned from hundreds of people who are experts in areas he aspires to master. Regardless of the difficulty, Josh now has someone he can call.

   "I've always been willing to help people, and as a result, it seems that all I have to do is ask and people are willing to help me," Josh explains.

   "I found these people," he said. "I sought them out, and it amazes me how many of them agreed to be available should I need them."

   With a contented smile, Josh concludes: "Having that kind of support frees you. It gives you a safety net for taking risks. It gives you freedom to be happy."

RUNNING ON HAPPINESS

A runner and her wheelchair-bound companion teach each other about happiness.

Jogging is very beneficial. It's good for your legs and your feet. It's also very good for the ground. It makes it feel needed.
—Charles M. Schulz

G o! Go, Yellow Power Ranger, go!" Boog shouted.

Sunny felt like she was pushing a Mack truck. Facing a sustained headwind is challenging enough for a distance runner, but pushing a child in a wheelchair 13.1 miles into a constant, strong, and steady wind can severely deplete your energy.

"Yellow Power Ranger . . . Hey, Miss Sunny!" Boog cried, "Go, go, go!"

Between huffing breaths, Sunny said, "We'll . . . make it . . . Red . . . Power Ranger."

Daryl McLane, aka Boog, was Sunny's captain for this race. Sunny was, therefore, Boog's angel. The wheelchair in which Boog rode is properly called a chariot. Boog and Sunny had been racing together regularly for more than a year, and after logging several dozen hours together on the road, they had become quite comfortable with each other.

"They're going to pass us," Boog warned.

Sunny glanced over at the man coming up steadily along their left side. The man's running shoes made a rhythmic *chauk, chauk, chauk* sound as they touched the pavement. The steady percussive sounds of his footfalls blended with the gentle *whirr* of the tires of the wheelchair he was pushing. The combination of sounds was like calming music to Sunny.

"Oh, they're not going to pass us," Sunny said.

"Oh, yes they are," little Boog responded peevishly.

"They might *think* so," teased Sunny as she leaned her head forward and added a sudden burst of speed. "Remember, kiddo," Sunny said in a conspiratorial stage whisper, "*we* have a secret weapon."

A wide grin spread across Boog's face. "Spiderman tattoos!" squealed Boog.

"Spiderman tattoos!" Sunny repeated.

Boog wondered if the temporary tattoo of his favorite superhero was still affixed to his cheek. In a similar situation, most boys Boog's age would have touched their cheek.

For Boog, that wasn't an option.

Boog was born with arthrogryposis. The word *arthrogryposis* means "curved joint," and it is a disease that causes children to be born with stiff and crooked joints. The range of motion for wrists, knees, hips, and other joints can be rigid or fixed. When explaining Boog's challenges with arthrogryposis, Sunny puts it succinctly: "It means that his arms and legs don't work.

"Doctors have tried everything on Boog," Sunny explained. "Surgery, brackets, contraptions, pins through his legs— everything to get his joints to work. He's three years old, and he can't walk, which means he can't run—unless I do the running for him."

Sunny and Boog were first paired up through Team Hoyt, which is named for Rick Hoyt and his father, Dick. Rick Hoyt was born in 1962 and was diagnosed as a spastic quadriplegic with cerebral palsy. His parents were advised to institutionalize Rick, but they refused. Dick and Judy Hoyt worked to integrate Rick into a society that, at that time, was more comfortable putting disabled people away so that they wouldn't be a hardship on their families.

When Rick turned fifteen, he told his dad that he wanted to run a 10K race (5.1 miles) to help raise money for a lacrosse player who had been paralyzed in an accident. Without giving much thought to how difficult it would be, Dick—who was not a runner—offered to push Rick's wheelchair. The two of them finished the race, coming in second to last.

That was only the beginning. Rick, the captain, and Dick— his father and angel—began to sign up for race after race, and in the process, they inspired runners to bring along wheelchair- bound children and smaller adults.

Sunny and Boog didn't always run together, but more often than not they did, and the pair had grown close. "When we run around the lake, Boog always has something to say about the geese," Sunny said with a laugh. "Or he's chattering along about his two favorite subjects: Power Rangers and Spiderman."

As Sunny walks up and down the aisles of the discount store looking for Spiderman tattoos and other goodies for Boog, she thinks about how happy she is and how important Boog is to her. The two have more in common than meets the eye.

Boog's physical ailments are apparent to everyone who meets him. Few can tell that Linda "Sunny" Fox—tall and fit as she is—has been battling thyroid cancer for more than half a decade.

"When I found out I was sick, it was surreal," Sunny described. "My husband had been battling cancer for more than a year when I began to feel tired all the time. I noticed I had a lump in my throat. I went to the doctor and found out that I, too, had cancer."

After a long moment, Sunny continued, "When they told me I was sick, I made a commitment to myself to run one thousand races." Linda shot a crooked smile and added, "Many is the time I've been in a race and caught myself wondering, *what was I thinking?*"

Since her commitment to run one thousand races, Sunny—either alone, with Boog, or with another captain—has completed eight marathons, more than twenty half marathons, and everything in between.

This past weekend, Sunny and Captain Boog completed another 5K, bringing Sunny's total number of races up to 366. Even though pushing Boog's chariot slows her down a couple of minutes per mile, Sunny—now age fifty-six—won the race for her age group. Sunny quips, "I might be running some day at age ninety-five, and I'll be the only one in my age group. And winning, even if it's by attrition, is great."

Sunny is grateful for Boog and even for her illness because they both remind her that no matter what life brings, being happy is a choice.

Sunny offers three suggestions for maintaining happiness.

1. **Remember that there is always someone who has it much worse than you:** "I have cancer, but they're going to cure me; at least my legs work so I can push Boog," Sunny says.

2. **Do nice things for other people:** Sunny says, "I think working with the Team Hoyt family makes us happier when we're out there helping the kids. We all know we're out there helping each other."

3. **Exercise regularly:** In addition to the endorphin rush of a runner's high, exercise has many other benefits that make you feel happier. "Just to feel that I'm in the best shape I can possibly be in and to be a role model for others make me feel happy," Sunny says.

When going through her cancer treatments, Sunny still runs as much as she can. She says, "Even though I feel crappy, I'll feel crappier if I don't work out first thing in the morning."

Happiness is born of a happy mind-set. Cultivate a happy mind-set by remembering that there are always those who have it worse than you, by doing nice things for others, and by making the time to exercise.

Being happy is a marathon, not a sprint.

HAPPY TO BE OF SERVICE

Team Hoyt: www.TeamHoyt.com

THE KEY TO
HAPPINESS

A key leads a woman on a search to discover the truth as well as the depth of her capacity to forgive and be happy.

Happiness depends upon ourselves.
—Aristotle

It started with a key.

As Betts walked through the Sears parking lot toward her car, she glanced down at the dozen or so keys on the ring in her hand. She was looking for the car key. On her own key ring, she didn't even have to look—she knew her car key by feel.

However, this wasn't Betts's key ring. These keys belonged to her husband, Omer. She had grabbed the wrong ones while running out the door.

Flipping through the keys, Betts came upon one she didn't recognize. At first she let it pass through her fingers as she continued her search. Without really knowing why, she flipped back to the unfamiliar key.

Betts looked at the key for a long moment. It seemed fairly new.

Arriving at her car, Betts held up the keys to unlock the door, and that same key glinted in the sunlight. Again, she studied it.

Betts turned and walked back toward Sears. Her mind spilled forth a mixed stew of questions and conjecture, including:

It looks like an apartment key. What would an apartment key be doing on my husband's key ring?

The key could be an old key that he just forgot to throw way. If that were true, why am I just now noticing it? And why does it look fairly new?

It could be a key for his work. It doesn't look like a work key.

It's just a key. Yes, but why am I getting such a strong feeling that this is important?

She realized after the fact that she had asked the question aloud.

"Can I help you?" a young man behind the customer service counter asked with a smile.

"I'd like a copy of this," Betts said, thrusting her hand out with the key in her upturned palm.

When he'd finished, the young man handed the new key to Betts. Something inside warned her against mentioning her copy of the key to anyone.

Over the next several weeks, what had seemed typical behavior for Omer began to appear suspicious. One night, as Betts prepared dinner, the phone rang. After listening to the receiver for a minute, she said flatly, "You're working late . . . again?"

"Hey, overtime is good money," Omer replied, parroting the same response he had used so many times.

Betts sat alone in the dark for a long time. Suddenly, she stood up, grabbed her purse, and walked out the front door.

Betts pulled her car up to the guard gate at Omer's place of employment.

"May I help you?" the guard inquired.

"Where are the lights?" Betts asked, sweeping her hand in the direction of the dark parking lot.

"Lights, ma'am?"

"The parking lot lights for the people working overtime."

The guard thought a moment. "Ma'am," he said, "we haven't had any employees working overtime here in more than two years."

It was not a puzzle she wanted completed, and yet here it was—another piece had fallen into place. Betts fingered the key as she drove home. The tears burned as they streamed down her cheeks. Still, Betts said nothing to Omer.

Five hundred dollars to a private detective provided ample evidence of Omer's infidelity.

A few days after she read the heartbreak of the detective's report, Omer called again informing Betts that he was working late. Betts waited several hours and then quietly left their house.

Arriving at the address provided by her PI, Betts walked up to the door and heaved a big sigh. She withdrew the key—the key that had started it all—and inserted it silently into the lock. There was a soft click, and Betts gently slid the door open.

Betts reached into her purse and withdrew a flashlight. She walked throughout the darkened apartment, crisscrossing each room with the beam of her flashlight. When she arrived at the closed door at the far left along the hall, she threw it open.

Betts's flashlight first illuminated the form of the other woman as she shrieked in fear and tugged the covers up under her chin. Then, panning the light to the right, Betts saw him. There he was—scrambling, screaming, threatening, blinded by the flashlight that shown into his eyes.

"You low-down *scum!*"

Omer knew her voice well. He also knew that his mistakes had just erased the sand castle of lies in which he had found solace.

In the wavering beam of her flashlight, Betts could see Omer struggle to cover his nakedness with a sheet.

"I need to speak with you," Betts said sternly but without a trace of anger. Omer refused to climb naked from the bed. Even though Betts had seen his naked body thousands of times over the past dozen years of marriage, standing nude before his wife and his lover was too much honesty for him.

Much later, Omer and Betts talked.

And then they talked some more. They talked for hours over a period of weeks before making a decision to separate. No one in Betts's family had ever been divorced. The word had never been spoken and yet that's where Betts was headed.

Betts and her three daughters began to build a new life together.

That was in 1969. Today, at age eighty-four, Betts talks about the events leading up to her divorce as if she were discussing the weather. Betty "Betts" Rivét has long since released all of her anger and resentment toward Omer.

"It took time," Betts said. "And it wasn't easy. But I guess I got through it okay because people tell me that I seem to be the happiest person they know."

Looking back on eight decades of living, Betts offers these three suggestions for living a happy life:

1. **If it's in the past, leave it there:** Chances are that if a person has not betrayed you, someone will someday. When it occurs, it is heartbreaking, but the quickest way to mend a broken heart is to stop "scratching the wound" with resentful and angry thoughts. Accept what has happened and move on.

2. **Make the world a better place:** "And how do you make the world a better place?" Betts asks, excited as a child. "Make yourself a better person. Become someone that people want to be around. You have to think about people around you. Improving yourself isn't vain or selfish. Constantly making yourself better so that other people will benefit from being around you is actually thoughtful and generous."

3. **Feel fortunate:** Happy people often speak of the importance of gratitude, but Betts takes it one step further.

   This grandmother of eleven and great-grandmother of eleven more advises: "Rather than just thinking about what you're thankful for, feel the feelings of gratitude. Cultivate that feeling of being grateful for the things and people in your life."

   "I've had a wonderful life," Betts says, not giving any additional words or mental energy to her husband's indiscretion or even to the cancer that ravaged one of her breasts, causing it be removed in 2011.

   "I've gone through a lot of things. But I'm wonderful—I feel happy."

   Betts leans forward to indicate the significance of her final piece of advice: "Don't look back—always look ahead."

A HOME FOR HAPPINESS

A man winds up homeless with his two sons and discovers what's really important.

Stay, stay at home, my heart, and rest;
Home-keeping hearts are happiest,
For those that wander they know not where
Are full of trouble and full of care;
To stay at home is best.
—Henry Wadsworth Longfellow

---

t's not supposed to be this hard, Robert thought to himself as he walked away from the homeless shelter.

Robert Schofield, age thirty-seven, had just been denied assistance from the third of three homeless shelters he had visited that day.

Robert sighed and trudged on. He wasn't exactly sure where to go next. Robert's two teenage sons—Robert IV, age fourteen, and Jeremiah, age thirteen—shuffled along behind him in robotic lockstep. Robert could feel his sons' disappointed looks burning into the back of his neck.

The trio was pacing more than walking. When you have nowhere to go, you're rarely in a hurry. The heat and humidity were stifling, but through repeated exposure they had become numb to St. Petersburg's summer swelter.

In the span of just three months, life had scrambled Robert like an egg. The ripples of the housing bust finally toppled Robert's company. The company had made a fortune in cell tower construction, and then they made a poor choice. In a hubris-induced state brought on by a sudden and dramatic influx of cash, Robert's company had switched to building high-end condos. They had made the switch at the worst possible time.

Robert, a truck driver for the company, was let go, and he began immediately to search for work. He soon found himself caught in the middle of the 2009 global recession; he faced serious challenges getting a job in a glutted job market.

Robert became stressed; his second wife became anxious and afraid. They argued.

One day Robert came home after looking for work to find that his wife had left, taking their young daughter with her.

Robert was crushed. "I've always been a producer," he said. "I've always worked. Now, I didn't have a job and couldn't find a job. Plus, my wife walked out with my baby girl."

Robert thought life had taken him to the basement, but he soon found out that there were even lower levels awaiting him.

"I don't care!" Robert's first wife screamed as he tried to explain how difficult life was for him at the moment. "I really don't care!" she repeated, shoving her two sons in Robert's direction. "I raised those boys for nearly thirteen years. They're your kids, too. They're yours to deal with now."

The boys, now nearly as tall as Robert, stared at their father in silence. Robert turned and walked back inside, the boys trailing like ducklings.

Before Robert's sons could settle into their new home, they discovered it was no longer theirs. Robert's estranged second wife had taken most of their possessions, and when he could no longer afford his rent, Robert and his sons took to the streets.

Robert III, Robert IV, and Jeremiah canvassed every church, homeless shelter, and aid-program office they could find. But they were always turned away empty-handed.

Robert discovered that there is a hierarchy to homelessness. When it comes to programs to serve the indigent, homeless women with children have the best odds of receiving assistance. Next comes homeless women with no children, followed by homeless men with no children. The group of homeless citizens least likely to receive aid and assistance is Robert's group—homeless men with children.

Robert couldn't understand how he could have fallen this far. And the way things were going, he could see no way of ever recovering.

Someone recommended yet another organization that offered help to the indigent, and Robert contacted them. Beginning to feel like he was simply going through the motions, Robert was shocked out of his malaise when he heard the program staff was willing to consider helping him.

Resurrection House of Florida is a nonprofit community that offers turnaround programs for adults. This dedicated organization teaches life skills to those who most sorely need them, including how to parent, budget money, and get and hold a job.

Resurrection House provides housing—but with a twist.

When a family is ready to buy a home—often for the first time—all of the furnishings from their Resurrection House dwellings go with them. Everything—from the beds and linens all the way down to the coffee maker—is theirs to keep. The family takes all of their furnishings to help make a smooth transition to their new lives and build a feeling of successful continuity.

The woman smiled compassionately as she handed Robert the application and overview of Resurrection House.

You will learn to create a household budget, be helped to get a job, and then you will account for everything you spend, comparing your expenses to your budget.

There is a strict curfew—no exceptions.

Children under the age of twelve must be with a parent at all times. This means, if you step outside for any reason, your children must be with you.

All children will attend school as well as tutoring classes twice each week.

Robert filled out the application and was accepted. He and his boys moved into their new home and were soon joined by Robert's estranged wife and daughter.

Robert found a job, too—one he loves and excels at. Robert is now the campus coordinator for Resurrection House. "Basically, I'm here to do whatever needs to get done," Robert said. "But my real job is often just to listen or offer a kind word."

Robert offers three happiness suggestions.

1. **Remember that you were born to be happy:** "We are born happy," Robert says. "Life beats us down, but kids are happy."
2. **Discover and appreciate who you are:** "If I could give my kids one piece of advice," Robert said, "it would be to learn

who you are as a person. It took me thirty-six years to learn who I am as a person and to be comfortable with that."

"It's amazing to me," Robert said with a bewildered grin. "I see so many people on these self-improvement kicks trying to fix something that may not even be broken."

3. **Stop worrying:** Robert grows animated when talking about how much people worry.

    "Most people worry, waiting on something to happen or not happen," Robert said, his voice rising with passion. "Me, I'm not going to worry until I get the response. If it makes sense to worry once I've seen how it worked out, I'll worry.

    "We run around like it's the end of the world," he said. "We have such a short memory." Sweeping his hands in a wide arc, Robert concluded with a smile: "You've made it through every other crisis. What makes you think you're not going to get through this one?"

HAPPY TO BE OF SERVICE

Florida Resurrection House:
www.FloridaResurrectionHouse.com

THE LIGHT OF HAPPINESS

A child performer from the Chop Suey Circuit grows up to discover happiness.

I mohala no ka lehua i ke ke'ekehi 'ia e ka ua.
(The lehua blossom unfolds when the rain treads on it.)
—Hawaiian proverb

"Time to shine little star," Pooki Lee's mother cooed, waking her with the same words she had used to rouse her child several times a night, five nights every week, for more than a decade.

Still dreaming, Pooki's twelve-year-old body stumbled from her cramped sleeping perch nestled against the back of the stage. Pooki's eyes remained closed, savoring a few more seconds of sleep. Besides, she didn't need to see. Her body knew the way.

Walking as if she were awake, Pooki strolled unconsciously with the precise cadence necessary to break through the door on cue. The moment her small hand pressed the brass doorplate and she opened wide the door, Pooki transformed.

As the buzzing stage lights bathed her once more in their warmth, Pooki's face—which only seconds before had been slack with sleep—spread wide as her enormous smile exploded, and her eyes popped open.

I might as well have stayed asleep, Pooki thought.

Her body had long since memorized every step, every pause, and every choreographed movement of the dance created for her by her mother and her grandmother. Pooki floated through her performance, barely aware of the people, the music, the blue haze of cigarette smoke, or the greasy smell of Americanized Chinese food.

Pooki started as a dancer on what was known as the Chop Suey Circuit when she was two years old. A decade later, she was continuing to dance alongside her mother and grandmother five nights a week in addition to going to school full-time.

Many American soldiers had returned from World War II missing the sweet and spicy food they had eaten in the Pacific Rim. Over the next couple of decades, Chinese and Polynesian restaurants began to pop up across the United States.

When once there were only one or two Chinese or Polynesian restaurants in a city, by the mid-1960s and 1970s there were dozens. Savvy restaurateurs set themselves apart by hiring performers to play music and dance for the dinner crowd.

Typically, a family of performers would arrive in town and be hired to perform at a local restaurant to increase business. Over time, however, sales would fall off because patrons would grow tired of seeing the same act over and over.

The performers would be fired and new entertainers would be brought in to revive the dinner business. The act that was released would float into another town to solicit work. This was life on the Chop Suey Circuit.

A couple of times a night, Pooki would dance the hula center stage while her mother and grandmother swayed rhythmically on either side of her.

Pooki described: "We'd hit town and my mother would cajole the owner of a local Asian restaurant to give us a try. If we were a hit, we stayed a while. If not, we were on our way."

With a smile both nostalgic and wistful, Pooki adds, "By the time I was fourteen, I had lived in more than fifty cities. Looking back on it," Pooki recalled, "dancing all the time wasn't easy, but I loved it. I absolutely loved it. In fact, it was the only part of the day when I felt appreciated and valued."

Because of their incessant relocating, Pooki was always the new kid in town.

"You've heard people say, 'I'm an army brat. When I was a kid, my family would be in a new city every year.' Well, we'd sometimes be in a new city every month or even more frequently. If we were a hit, we'd stay in a town for a year, but that wasn't the norm."

Children develop deep and lasting bonds with their friends. Some of these relationships will endure for a lifetime. However, developing these close associations takes time, and when you're not around for very long, the odds are against you to make any deep and lasting friendships.

Having no history upon which to build an affinity group to offer friendship and support, Pooki was teased mercilessly. Her broad, attractive smile—which today, at age fifty-two, has been likened to that of Mick Jagger or Carol Burnett—caused her to receive numerous hurtful comments as a teenager.

"Lippy the Lion, they called me," Pooki said. "I don't even know what that means. But back then it hurt."

And then there was the question of her ethnicity.

"I wasn't white—people could see that," Pooki explained. "But I certainly wasn't black. I'm not quite brown, and I don't look like I'm Asian. Kids didn't know how to label me and that frustrated them. It wasn't easy being a member of an indistinguishable ethnic group living in the Midwest during the 1960s."

For the record, Pooki is Polynesian.

When Pooki became a spindly and awkward teenager, her mother and grandmother saw that she could no longer be the cute little novelty component for their act. Pooki was sent to live with an aunt who suffered from severe depression and other mental illnesses.

Although happy to be in a town long enough to develop friendships, Pooki missed her mother and grandmother, as well as the adulation she received from performing.

In addition to an unusual and challenging childhood, Pooki has experienced difficulty as an adult, having been homeless twice.

And yet, if you ask anyone who knows her—for that matter, if you ask anyone who has ever met Pooki—they will tell you that when you're around her, you feel happy energy surging out as bright as the sun.

How has Pooki moved from a difficult childhood to becoming a radiant beam of happiness? Pooki offers three things that work for her.

1. **Shift your focus:** If we constantly focus on ourselves, we find a black hole that always wants more—more money, more status, more fitness, more friends, more everything. This hole

can never be filled. The quickest way to shift from emptiness to fullness is to want other people to be happy.

When your intention for everyone is that they be happy, you shift your focus away from yourself, and this quiets that "never enough" internal voice. Plus, everyone you come in contact with feels your positive intention, and they let down their defenses. Fewer defenses means less defensiveness. Less defensiveness means fewer disagreements.

When your focus is on what will make your family and friends happy, you are giving, which adds value to the relationship. When you focus on what you can get from your family and friends that you think will make you happy, you are taking—which diminishes the value of the relationship.

2. **Stay close to the light:** Pooki has never forgotten the simple thrill of standing beneath a spotlight and having a small audience shower her with gratitude and admiration.

There is a small group of people who are emotionally capable to want only the best for you and to accept you in all your idiosyncratic human glory without any changes, whatsoever. There is an even smaller group of people who can do this and who also find you fascinating and appealing. Interact with this group as often as possible.

Happiness and self-esteem are proportional. The better you feel about yourself, the happier you are.

"I get up every morning, and I get excited that I get to be me for another twenty-four hours!" Pooki gushed. This isn't vanity. Vanity is believing that you are the center of the universe, whereas accepting appreciation and approval is savoring the sunlight that shines your way.

3. **Happiness breeds happiness:** "When you start living happiness, you attract other people who are happy, and this brings

around more happy people," said Pooki, her smile radiating equal warmth from her eyes and her wide grin.

Happiness is like a perpetual motion machine. Once you get it started, it just runs and runs.

THE LANGUAGE OF HAPPINESS

In Hawaiian, the word for happy is *hauʻoli* (how-O-lee).

FREE TO BE HAPPY

A family risks everything to be free and happy.

The secret of happiness is freedom. The secret of freedom is courage.
—Thucydides

Dámelo a mi"* ("Hand him to me"), Francisco Urbina whispered, extending his arms toward his eldest son.

"Yo lo tengo" ("I've got him"), Xavier said, his thick exhalation causing the words to come out louder than they should, given his family's situation. Xavier, only thirteen years of age, had been carrying his three-year-old brother Omar on his back for nearly three hours.

Xavier leaned forward and dipped his left shoulder to shift Omar's little body, distributing his weight more evenly. Out of the corner of his eye, Xavier could see his mother, Mily, silhouetted in the moonlight. Before him, his father Francisco's thirty-two-year-old body stood hunched over, with hands on his knees as he breathed heavily. To Xavier, his father looked decades older than he had only a week before.

Their timing was precise. There was just enough moonlight to see, but not enough moonlight to be seen. This was the final step. Either it would happen or it would not. If they failed, it could mean death for them all. If they succeeded, it meant finally being free of persecution.

This small family of four was about to cross the Rio Grande to the United States. A combination of wading and swimming through one hundred meters of muddy water was all that remained of their flight. They had already made it on foot and off the grid from Mexico City.

Carrying Omar had been the most difficult across the hot, shifting sands of the Sonoran Desert, which they had chosen as their route north to lessen the likelihood of being detected.

Along their journey, Xavier and his father took turns carrying Omar, who walked on his own only occasionally. Mily trudged silently along only a few steps behind. As she walked, she prayed.

And now . . . now she could see in the distance a ghostly haze of lights projected into the night sky above El Paso. Mily's prayers were nearly fulfilled.

For a decade, the Urbina family had experienced threats and harassment in their native Mexico. Over the years, the tactics of fear and intimidation had grown in frequency and intensity.

A political struggle is a struggle for power between factions. Those caught in between are either swept up on one side or become collateral damage.

"The Mexican government does a good job of covering it up," says Xavier. "Mexico does a lot of business with the United States. If people knew the extent of the unrest and oppression going on there, they would demand changes be made."

Power does not like change because change threatens power.

"I was born in Mexico City," recounts Xavier in flawless English. "Because my father was from southern Mexico and refused to comply with the mandatory requirement that every man register with the military, the government thought we were rebels. But because my father also refused to sign on with the rebels, they thought we were on the government's side. Both the rebels and the government feel that if you don't publicly proclaim your allegiance to them, then you are against them."

Xavier takes a moment to breathe, adding: "I've asked my father if he ever received any threats or torture from either side." Xavier's voice drops to a compassionate whisper: "But every time I bring it up, he breaks down. So we just don't talk about it anymore."

When Xavier was ten, the rebels began making creeping inroads into Mexico City. Always undermanned, the rebels enlisted young men to join their cause.

"Not long after I turned thirteen," Xavier said, "I was approached by two rebel soldiers. They asked me to join the resistance. They told me they would give me a gun and pay me. 'Together, we'll stand up to the government,' they said."

Then, as the rebels' cause became more desperate, they traded enrollment for capture. Brandishing guns, rebel soldiers burst into parents' homes and kidnapped their young sons. The boys were taken to rebel camps to be trained under threat of death. They were later forced to kill—including friends and neighbors.

Xavier was one of ten adolescent boys in his neighborhood. In one night, seven disappeared.

The morning after the mass kidnappings, Francisco sipped his coffee with trembling hands and stared at Xavier. Almost as if he were accidentally speaking his words aloud, he said, "Before you get taken away, let's go to the United States."

When they arrived north of the border, the family did odd jobs to survive. They were free from fear for the first time in years. But then, a realization caused them to augment their plans.

If they were caught as illegal immigrants in the United States, they would be immediately deported back to Mexico. In Mexico, both sides would take their escape attempt as an indication of guilt and would ramp up their attacks.

However, if they continued on into Canada and were discovered as being illegal, they could select the country to which they would be deported.

The Urbina family migrated to Windsor, Ontario, where they now all have steady jobs. Within a year of arriving in North America, fourteen-year-old Xavier became fluent in English to act as a translator for his mother and father.

This illegal immigrant teenager became president of his high school class and captain of the soccer team. He has earned several awards from the school board. Most significantly, the Canadian Minister of Education placed Xavier Urbina at the top of the list of young leaders in Canada.

Xavier, now age twenty-two, works for the Winter Refugee Office, an extension of the Diocese of London, Ontario—the very organization that helped him and his entire family obtain permanent residency in Canada.

To know Xavier is to know his smile. It's as if his smile, itself, were on a mission. Xavier wakes up each morning with a beaming smile that shines into the world and leads him through his day. He is happiness personified.

Here are Xavier's three suggestions for being happy:

1. **Believe in the impossible:** "When I approach a situation that is tough," Xavier says, "I lay it in God's hands, knowing that He will do it. Instead of being sad about the situation, I

approach it as a new experience. I approach it as one more thing to learn in life."

2. **Hold an intention:** "In Mexico, there is a saying, 'It may be raining at night, but the sun comes in the morning.'" Xavier says. "Instead of focusing on the problem, what is the end you would like to see? Keep your focus on that."

3. **Smile . . . always smile:** "We all smile in the same language," Xavier said, his face making his point. "You never know whose life you can change with a smile. If you approach life with a smile, you're showing strength and you're showing optimism, and this world is missing that. If you can smile in the toughest time of your life, everything else is smooth and easy."

THE LANGUAGE OF HAPPINESS

In Spanish, the word for happy is *feliz* (feh-LEEZ).

BLOOM WHERE YOU ARE PLANTED

A stranger's greetings transform an entire town.

How far we travel in life matters far less than those we meet along the way.
—American saying

That year, a young disabled girl began to connect with other people for the first time.

That year, the high school girl's field hockey team went to state.

That year, a middle-aged woman bent on suicide made another choice.

That year, the people of Greenwich, New York, all felt happier.

Greenwich is a picturesque small town of about eighteen hundred, where everyone knows or is related to everyone else. It is difficult to describe Greenwich without using words such as *quaint* and *charming*.

That year—that very special year for Greenwich—all began when one man decided to do something a little different.

Lorenzo Ross had returned to Greenwich for the third summer in a row to work for a company that was hired to lay new gas pipes throughout the town. Lorenzo worked as a flagman for the construction team. For twelve to fifteen hours a day, Lorenzo stood in one place and directed drivers around the roadwork.

"I see them going to work and coming home every day." Lorenzo said, "You get to where you know every car. You know the people." Lorenzo's words were punctuated by short bursts of gleeful laughter. "One day I just had an idea. I'm standing there. I have to have something pleasant to think about. Why don't I just wave at everybody who goes by?"

And he did. Lorenzo waved at every driver, pedestrian, and skateboarder that passed his way. At first, nobody waved back.

"No one responded!" Lorenzo said, still laughing. "I kept saying hello to every car that went by and smiling at everybody."

On the second day, however, a few hands fluttered waves back. By the third day, some people actually waved at Lorenzo before he had a chance to wave at them.

And from there, it grew.

Lorenzo, who had been performing this same job in the same town for six months of the previous two years, simply decided to make a connection with everyone who passed him. Soon, rather than avoiding the construction site, people in Greenwich began to drive out of their way to be slowed down and greeted by Lorenzo. Some even got out and exchanged hugs with him.

And Lorenzo got into it. For a dozen hours or more each day, Lorenzo would smile and wave and shout out well wishes. He became everyone's "morning coffee" to start the day, as well as their calming "glass of wine" at day's end.

One day as their school bus passed on the way to a game, the girls in the high school field hockey team—every last one—reached out the bus window to high-five Lorenzo. The team won and credited Lorenzo with their success. From that day forward, the girls insisted that they be driven by Lorenzo for high-fives before each game. The girls ultimately made it to the state finals.

On another day as Lorenzo waved traffic forward on one side of the road—using an overly dramatic gesture one might reserve for royalty—a young mother lowered her car window and called his name. Lorenzo approached the car to see a friendly woman with a small child strapped in the back.

"You helped her," the mother said.

"Ma'am?"

The woman was excited to be speaking to Lorenzo in person for more than a fleeting pass. "My daughter," she said. "She was born disabled. She never developed the ability to focus on people's faces. One day, we were waiting for you to move cars along, and I noticed she was watching you. Soon after, I noticed that she was starting to focus on my face and other people's faces, too."

Tears rolling down her cheeks, the woman extended her hand and said in a voice constricted by emotion, "Thank you, Lorenzo."

Lorenzo held her hand for a moment, smiled, and then waved her past.

Another woman, distraught by the pain of living, was on her way home to end her life when Lorenzo raised his hand to stop her vehicle. The woman was distracted from ruminating about her "hopeless" and "empty" life by the big bear of a man leaping about, smiling and gesturing warmly to everyone. Here was a man who was standing in the hot sun all day—separated by steel and glass from people—and yet he had found a way to get into their lives and into their hearts.

For the first time, the woman saw that life is about what we give and not what we get. She went home and made a decision to get out of her own problems and into helping others.

Then, there were the gifts people brought to Lorenzo. "One day an elderly woman brought me some cookies," Lorenzo said, savoring the memory. "Then, another lady also brought cookies. Then someone noticed I was in the hot sun and gave me a bottle of water."

Lorenzo stopped talking so that he could laugh for several minutes. When he could speak again, he said, "Man . . . I got so much water, I'd give bottles to everybody on the crew and still go home with a full case at the end of the night.

"Whenever the pizza guy would go by, he'd take my order and bring me back pizzas—free pizzas! The crew loved it! I was always passing out slices of pizza, cans of soda, cookies—you name it, people were giving it to me, and I shared it with the gang."

Sadly, all good things—even road construction, traffic tie-ups, and detours—must come to an end. As mid-December approached, the people of Greenwich were happy that Santa Claus would soon be arriving, but they were equally sad that Lorenzo would soon be leaving.

In a public ceremony, the city of Greenwich designated Lorenzo Ross an honorary citizen, and the mayor presented him with a key to the city.

You may not be fortunate enough to meet Lorenzo as he smiles through your windshield, but you can learn a lot from his three tips for happiness.

1. **Put a smile on your face:** "Smiling lets you relax," says Lorenzo. "We go through our daily journeys and things can get rough. When we smile, we release that energy. We're not as tense and upset."

   Through his hundred-watt smile, Lorenzo adds: "Smiling lets me not think about things that are going to steal my joy. My smile keeps me connected with my joy."

2. **Stop stressing about things over which you have no control:** "If you can do something about it," Lorenzo advises, "do it. If there's nothing you can do, you might as well give it to God and just trust that it's going to work out."

3. **Move past the pain:** Two years ago, Lorenzo's twenty-two-year-old son died of asthma. Lorenzo was grief stricken. However, he has worked to shift his focus away from his son's death to remembering and celebrating the good things from his life.

Few townspeople anxiously anticipate road construction. But, then again, few towns have had the privilege of getting to know Lorenzo Ross.

THE PRIVILEGE OF
BEING HAPPY

An Amish man shares simple tips for happiness.

When we are unhurried and wise, we perceive that only great and worthy things have any permanent and absolute existence.
—Henry David Thoreau

L et's sit over here," John said, motioning toward the front porch of his house. "It's cooler out here. And you're used to air-conditioning."

Minutes earlier, as I turned from the dirt road into John's driveway, my car's external temperature display had read 107 degrees.

John Kurtz, age sixty-one, had been sorting cucumbers for pickling when I arrived. He strode toward me, smiling warmly. He wore a handmade long-sleeve work shirt the color of mushrooms, handmade jeans, suspenders, gradient tint bifocals, a straw hat, and boots. John's upper lip was shaved smooth, and his bushy white sideburns converged into a long gray beard.

"I don't really have much to say," John said, taking a seat.

The summer wind stroked the green leaves of the crops planted in front of John's home. Rippling emerald waves rolled up the hill to where John and I sat on his porch.

Nellie, John's dapple-gray mare, stood fully tacked, dozing at a hitching post in nearby shade. John had plans to ride her later to check the crops.

Through the open window came a *slursh, slursh, slursh* sound as a woman whistled what sounded like a hymn.

"She doesn't churn it," John said, answering my unasked question. His eyes were the same color as the cloudless Missouri summer sky behind him. "That sound is my wife, Emma, making butter. She doesn't use a churn. She puts milk in a jug and shakes it."

The whistling stopped. "Cream," Emma corrected from inside the kitchen.

"What?" asked John.

"You said milk," Emma said. "I make butter from cream."

Emma walked out onto the porch and extended a solid handshake along with a broad, welcoming smile. After some pleasantries, she withdrew to the kitchen to get John and me a glass of ice water, served, of course, in a mason jar with hand-chipped ice.

John and I sipped the water and savored the breeze that made the summer heat bearable.

"You're the first Amish person I've ever spoken to," I admitted.

John smiled and nodded his head. He was used to being a curiosity. "My first language is German," he said. "We all speak and pray in German. So I may have trouble saying much in English that you can use."

Across the street, there was a bustle of activity at the school. The teachers inside the sweltering concrete-and-tin structure were preparing for the twenty-five or so children from this Amish district who would head back to school in August. A buggy sat parked behind the school. Not far away, the buggy's equine drivetrain—a Belgian gelding—grazed beneath a sprawling oak tree.

"I guess I'll be moving to the doddy house soon," John said, continuing a conversation we'd not yet begun.

Seeing my perplexed expression, John explained: "Grandfather house . . . doddy house is the grandfather house."

If there is a house just for grandfathers, John would certainly qualify: he is the father of ten and grandfather of thirty-two.

"That's how it works," said John. "When you get older, you move into the doddy house. Then your youngest married child moves into your house."

"Who lived in the doddy house before you?" I asked.

"My father-in-law, Tobe Detweiler," he replied. "He ran a harness repair shop. He had a stroke at eighty-six and died at ninety-four."

Chickens scratched in the dirt nearby, and a rooster stood on its toes and flapped its wings, crowing loudly.

"His mind was still sharp," John said. "But he lost complete control of his body. It was my privilege to help care for him for the last seven years of his life."

PRIVILEGE?

John didn't say he had to take care of him. Nor did he say it was an ordeal, a hassle, or a struggle. He characterized assuming responsibility for an old man's physical needs for nearly 2,600 consecutive days as a *privilege*.

And the word *privilege* sums up John's perspective of life. It's one of the three tips for happiness that he offers.

1. **Notice how privileged you are:** John considers it a privilege to be the father of ten and grandfather of thirty-two. He considers it a privilege to be an ordained reverend in his church. He considers it a privilege to live in a country where he can live and be free as an Amish man.

    The word *privilege* is defined as a special right afforded one person or a limited group. Being a member of your family is a special right afforded to only a select few, therefore it is a privilege. Being the parent of your children is a special right afforded to only you and one other person; therefore it is a privilege. Having the job you have is a special right given only to a certain number. Your job, therefore, is a privilege.

    When you shift your life from "got to" to "get to" you remind yourself how privileged you are. When you begin to understand that millions of people alive today would gladly trade places with you at any time, you realize just how privileged you are.

    When you feel privileged, you feel happy because your focus is on your many blessings rather than your relatively few difficulties.

2. **Cultivate your spirituality:** There have been myriad studies connecting happiness with having a strong spiritual center. John nodded in agreement when I mentioned this to him.

    "Of course," he said, "you can't be happy if you are afraid and anxious all the time. Peace is the connection between spirituality and happiness. If you believe that there is something out there that is bigger than you, that loves you, that wants only the best for you, and that is working on your problems all of the time, you can relax, find peace, and be happy."

3. **Family comes first:** That evening, all of John's married children, their spouses, and all thirty-two of their children would be making the buggy ride to John and Emma's for a bonfire.

"No one lives more than five miles from the rest of the family," John said. "There is a lot of peace in having close family nearby.

"Again," John said, rising to give me a tour of his farm, "it comes down to peace. When you've got nearly sixty relatives that love you all within a thirty-minute ride in a horse and buggy, you feel peace. You feel blessed. You feel very, very privileged."

THE LANGUAGE OF HAPPINESS
In German, the word for happy is *fröhlich* (FROYE-lich).

HAPPY AT WORK

A woman changes careers to help young adults plan happier lives.

To laugh often and much; to win the respect of intelligent people and the affection of children; to earn the appreciation of honest critics and to endure the betrayal of false friends; to appreciate beauty; to find the best in others; to leave the world a bit better whether by a healthy child, a garden patch or a redeemed social condition; to know that even one life has breathed easier because you have lived. This is to have succeeded.
—Bessie A. Stanley

White noise.

It had all become white noise. Norma sat across the table from the fourteen-year-old who sprawled before her in her office guest chair. Norma stared through him as if he were an apparition.

Here he is: another child in an endless succession of children who have been arrested for assault.

Flavoring every sentence liberally with the *f* word, this angry, self-righteous man-child droned on incessantly about the need for earning and maintaining respect. "There's only so many times you can let a f***er f*** with you, right? I mean, f***!" Norma heard him say, realizing how desensitized she had become to profanity.

To say that Norma had heard it all before would be to imply that she still listened. It had become increasingly more difficult to listen to the cascade of justifications for violence and mayhem perpetuated by teenage males at the Brooklyn, New York, juvenile detention center every day.

Norma felt a strong calling to improve the world through her job. But she was beginning to question whether it was possible with *this* job.

"I decided it must just be because I'm working with boys," Norma recalls. "So I asked for a transfer to work with girls in a JD center in the Bronx."

Norma shakes her head slowly. "I thought girls would be different, you know? I thought that girls wouldn't be so prone to violence."

Norma pauses a moment. When she continues, her voice sounds disconnected—lifeless: "Then one day I was working with a ten-year-old girl. She was the sweetest little thing. Really adorable, you know?

"Well, this precious little girl, she . . . she was in the facility for killing another ten-year-old girl." After a deliberate breath, Norma continues with practiced restraint. "The other girl had taken her doll. That's all. Can you believe it? This girl took another little girl's doll and wound up dead."

Her eyes moist with tears, Norma shakes her head and breathes the word *dead* once more as if it were from a foreign language and she was trying, unsuccessfully, to become comfortable using it.

Norma realized that she had been fishing too far downstream. By the time children got to her, their patterns and environments were pretty well set.

Norma decided to take a leap from cure to prevention.

Decisions made by high school seniors are some of the most critical decisions a person will ever make. This is a time when people are not quite yet adults and not quite still children, but they make choices in setting a life course that can be difficult to alter in future years.

Norma felt that few students in her community had the full, loving support of their parents during this critical time. Desiring to bridge the gap between what students need and what parents are able to give, she made a career change and became a high school guidance counselor at Hillcrest High School in Jamaica, Queens, New York. A more diverse student body is hardly imaginable.

Smiling warmly, Norma says of her students: "They're little shining stars that don't know how to beam enough. My job is to help them really shine."

Most of Norma's students are from far-flung places such as Pakistan, Bangladesh, Jamaica, Haiti, and India. Many are African American, a few are Hispanic, and there are a handful of Caucasian kids. "Working with immigrant parents can be challenging," Norma explains. "They have heard for decades that the pinnacle of success is raising a son or daughter to become an American doctor.

"Not every child wants to become a doctor," Norma continues. "In fact, with the way the medical industry is shifting, sometimes a person can make more money and have a better financial future in another field."

Students will frequently come to Norma distraught. They want to pursue a degree other than medicine, and this desire creates conflict within the family. "I help the parents open their eyes and take a good look at the young man or woman they have raised thus far. I invite them to understand that being happy is more important than any particular job, and no matter how much money a person has, if he or she isn't fulfilled, it will never be enough."

Norma's friends, family, and colleagues consider Norma to be the happiest person they know. For a person who sees her role as helping others shine, she herself radiates happiness.

Norma offers three observations for becoming happier.

1. **Every day may not be a good day, but every day has something great in it:** Norma explains, "You wake up late because your alarm didn't go off, your hot water doesn't work, you get to work and your boss yells at you. At the end of the day, you could look back and call this a bad day. Or you could recall someone you helped, something you accomplished, or something new you experienced and discover that even this day had greatness in it."

2. **Find a job you love:** "In the middle of summer when I'm supposed to be on vacation, I'm working," says Norma. "I'm planning, researching, and for me all of this is fun!"

   No amount of money will justly compensate you for a life spent doing something you dislike. Every person has within them a predisposition to some field of endeavor. In today's world, where you can learn almost anything about nearly everything from the Internet, it is easier to follow your dreams than ever before.

3. **Develop contentment:** "On my office wall, I have this quote from Dr. Maya Angelou: *Success is liking yourself, liking what you do, and liking how you do it.*

"I never point it out to the students, but every now and then one will read and comment on it, and it's then that we really get to have some good conversations," Norma says.

Work on liking yourself. Become your own best friend, knowing that best friends neither judge nor do they berate the other person. Best friends appreciate and look past quirks and idiosyncrasies.

Do what you like to do. It's never too late to move toward doing for a living what you would gladly live to do. "I tell the parents of students that it's wonderful to have different goals, but ultimately they have to follow their heart," Norma says. "At the end of the day, you want them to be happy."

Like how you do your work. "The only way to like how you do your work," explains Norma, "is to do it the best you can."

Making a contribution by providing excellent service, regardless of your chosen field of endeavor, brings pride of accomplishment, and this leads to happiness.

Norma concludes: "I always tell the kids, 'Do something for yourself today that your future self will thank you for.' Every minute brings a chance to do something to improve ourselves. Having that kind of power to make things better for me and for others; that makes me happy."

THE LANGUAGE OF HAPPINESS

In countries where Arabic is the common language, Happy is a common surname for both male and female children. Boys are named *Sa'id* (sah-EED) and girls are named *Saida* (sah-EE-dah).

COLOR ME HAPPY

A man heals the wounds and missteps of his past to discover happiness and success.

It takes courage to grow up and become who you really are.
—E. E. Cummings

His friend didn't think anything of it. To Jeannie, the arrangement was perfect. Chad liked playing with her Barbies and she liked playing with his Hot Wheels. So, they switched. What could be better?

Every morning she would gulp down breakfast and rush over to his house. Kindergarten lay in their near future, and the highlight of their days was being together.

One day, three older boys passed by and stopped. When they saw Chad playing with a girl, they began to tease him. "They called me a pantywaist and a sissy," he says. "I'd never heard those words before, but, somehow, I knew what they meant. And, for some reason, I felt guilty . . . ashamed."

Chad Kenyon, now age forty-one, smiles as he continues: "I could barely count to ten, and I knew I was different. But I discovered that other kids could see it too. And it made some of them mean."

Lacon, Illinois, is just thirty minutes north of Peoria. In 1972, the year Chad was born, townspeople either worked for Caterpillar or they farmed. Being gay was not spoken of in polite company in rural America in the early 1970s. At that time, the word was primarily an insult boys and men threw at each other.

"My family loved me—I knew that," Chad shares. "We were very loving and touchy-feely. But it seemed like nobody quite knew how to take me for who I was, and so, like most gay people at that time, I denied the truth about myself.

"At school, I was even more confused. I could tell my classmates liked me—they elected me class president. But then they'd call me Dion like the flamboyantly gay stereotype Eddie Murphy played on *Saturday Night Live*.

"I felt like I was always being either lovingly caressed or wickedly slapped, and I never knew which was coming next."

Chad wished to go somewhere—anywhere that he could be himself and just be accepted for who he was.

While a senior in college, Chad got his wish. He received an ambassadorial scholarship to study in Spain. Spain immediately became his new home.

For the first time in his life, Chad lived where he was free to be himself. Madrid had a large and active gay community, and he became smitten with European culture and sophistication.

Chad fell in love both with the city and with a famous chef. Unfortunately, during their relationship that would span ten years, Chad spiraled down into the twin madnesses of excess and addiction.

"Together, we opened a restaurant in Chueca, which is at the very center of Madrid," says Chad. "We hoped to have a moderately successful place that appealed to a mostly gay clientele, but the restaurant caught on fast and soon we were booming. I suddenly had a dizzying amount of freedom and a pile of money to go with it. I had always felt off-balance, and now my life supported that vertigo. I got into what I like to call *messy diversions*. Messy diversions could and often did include drugs, orgies, and drinking until I passed out."

Chad pauses a moment and his voice softens to a whisper. "I wanted out of my head," he says, his eyes misting. "I was thousands of miles away from Lacon, and I could still feel the pain."

At twenty-four, Chad was diagnosed HIV positive.

"We didn't have the cocktail of drugs to keep us alive back then like we do now," Chad recalls. "An HIV diagnosis was a death sentence, and I reasoned if I'm dying anyway, I might as well really let loose." Shaking his head in disbelief at his own behavior, Chad explains, "In a single weekend, I'd do so much coke, I'd have to take thirty or so Ambien to take the edge off. Then there was all the drinking on top of it. I was typically barely conscious or passed out unconscious."

Chad's chef partner had lost a sister to drug addiction and could no longer bear to see his lover destroy himself, their business, and even his own career. At first they split up as a couple, attempting to try to stay together as business partners. Ultimately, however, Chad found himself unable to control his obsessions and signed everything over to his ex-lover. The restaurant they began, Divina la Cocina, remains a culinary landmark in Madrid.

Chad, desperate and destitute, called a friend in the United States, begging for help. The friend was able to get Chad placed into the Van Ness Recovery House in Hollywood, California.

"Recovery boot camp," says Chad. "They had a rigorous schedule you had to adhere to. Up every morning at six, prescribed times for meals and activities. Plus, we did all the work to keep the place going. We were required to be fully self-sustaining."

Chad worked diligently to heal the demons of his youth that set aflame the self-destruction of his adulthood. He finally realized that people tend to attack what they don't understand, and that the comments and jeers directed at him from others were in no way a reflection of him or his value. He accepts and is proud of himself now, and others respond to his newfound positive self-image.

Chad continues to work a program of recovery, and by all accounts has become a peaceful and happy guy. Plus, he's prospering doing something he loves—and it all came about as a result of his stint in rehab.

"One of the things Van Ness required is that we get a minimum wage job to humble ourselves," Chad says, flashing his wide smile. "I got a job at a hair salon and loved it. So I saved up and went to cosmetology school."

Chad is now a hair color expert at an exclusive salon in Beverly Hills. His wealthy and famous customers love the way he makes their hair look, but even more than that they love how Chad makes them feel. In addition to getting their color just so, Chad charges up his clients' happiness batteries with his positive and happy outlook.

Chad offers the following three happiness suggestions.

1. **Live your unique self:** We are constantly influenced by others who would like to help us define who we are. Most people are focused primarily on themselves, and, as such, they tend

to want you to look and act in a way that is most convenient for them.

To delve deeply into your own heart and ask the tough questions takes courage. It takes even more courage to live according to what you discover about yourself. "It's an ongoing process," says Chad. "I'm constantly peeling off the layers to discover the true version."

2. **Get in touch with a higher vibration:** Throughout time, great spiritual masters have all meditated.

    Meditation is becoming mainstream for a very good reason. It reduces stress, lowers blood pressure, increases focus, and quiets the mind. Chad considers meditation a must for being happy. "I ask the universe to give me intuitive thoughts and to give me signs so I can make adjustments in my behavior and attitudes," he says. "If I feel I'm guided in my life and am always improving, I'm happy."

3. **Forget about yourself:** In many ways, happiness is a lack of obsessing about yourself and your problems. When you stop ruminating about yourself, you free yourself to feel happy.

    Chad volunteers his time to help others who are facing the same problems he faced. "When I'm focused on someone else," he says, "I can't be stressing out about myself."

    Oh, and remember Jeannie, Chad's childhood friend? More than three decades later they're still close. "Chad's the happiest guy I know," says Jeannie. "And I love him."

THE LANGUAGE OF HAPPINESS

In Spanish, the word for happiness is *felicidad* (feh-LEEZ-see-dahd).

LIVING HAPPY

A boy survives starvation in China and grows to help feed others.

The virtuous man is driven by responsibility; the non-virtuous man is driven by profit.
—Confucius

ould this be the day? Jai Yu wondered to himself.

Jai Yu was small for a boy. His lean body moved with each step like a reed in rippling currents. As he walked with head down, carefully balancing his steps along the bank of the parched earth that had once been a rice paddy, the dust puffed up through the toes of his leathery feet.

"Yes," he said aloud. "Today could be the day. In fact, it *must* be the day." A smile rounded his long face: "Yes, today it is. No doubt about it."

He trudged forward.

Jai Yu's life was simultaneously monotonous and unrelenting. He worked constantly and yet always seemed to be behind. Now, as he slogged through the mud, the bamboo pole dug into the calloused crests of his narrow shoulders. The two pails, each suspended on one end of the pole's tips, sloshed away a little precious water with each of his steps. Jai Yu was walking home, having collected water for the first, but by no means the last, time that day. It was at times like this, painful, mind-numbing times like this, that he allowed himself to play what he called the If Today Were My Birthday game.

If today is the day, he thought, *my mother will be cleaning and hanging lanterns.*

Nodding his head in agreement with his own thoughts, he thought some more: *If today is my birthday, my mother will be cooking long noodles for me.* He imagined his mother standing over their cook pot as it billowed fragrant steam, and she carefully folded extra-long noodles into its cavernous belly.

He said aloud, "I will fill my mouth with as many noodles as I can. Only when I cannot hold any more will I bite down. Thus, I will be assured a long and prosperous life."

His every sense was stirred by the mental mirage of spicy, savory, succulent noodles. Jai Yu's mouth began to salivate.

Jai Yu played the If Today Were My Birthday game for two reasons: First, thinking about a fancy birthday feast wherein he would eat until his stomach ached took his mind away from the ravenous demon of hunger that constantly gnawed at him. Never in his life had he enough to eat, so his grandest wish was to someday—if only once—have more than enough food at a meal.

The second reason he played the If Today Were My Birthday game is that any day might indeed be his birthday. In rapid succession, his mother bore ten children of which Jai Yu was the second born. When he came along, his mother had been too busy to make note of Jai Yu's date of birth. He knew the year was 1948. That was all he knew.

Jai Yu went to sleep each night with his stomach gnarled from hunger. When he awoke each morning, he would arise and strap one of his younger siblings to his back.

"I can't remember a time when my back wasn't wet," Jai Yu says. "I always had one of them strapped to me. Well, infants do what infants do, and my back was always wet." Jai Yu shifts back and forth in his seat almost imperceptibly as he says, "I'm sixty-five, and I still feel like my back is wet sometimes."

While other boys played and climbed trees, Jai Yu cooked, cleaned the house, and took care of his eight brothers and their one sister.

It had been a time of great famine in China, and Jai Yu was well acquainted with the ravages of starvation. "I would be following grazing cattle, and as I passed people's homes there would be small mounds of fresh dirt at the edge of their fields," he said, the six-decade-old memory still fresh and painful in his mind. "These were the graves of small children hastily buried in bamboo vegetable baskets. They were everywhere."

Jai Yu pauses, clears his throat, and says, "We were all so hungry. Everything just seemed hopeless."

When he was old enough to support himself, Jai Yu had to leave home to make room for his brothers and sister who were growing up and needing more space in their cramped home.

"It was the best thing for everyone," he says, his smile continuing to expand. "I worked wherever I could, and as I did I observed our communal way of living. Everyone was supposed to produce and share equally in all production. Communal living is a wonderful ideal so long as there is no one skimming off the top."

Throughout China at that time, there were a great many officials at every level profiting from the deprivation and starvation of others.

Jai Yu banded people together to push for the privatization of land. Rather than sharecropping at a very high interest rate, farmers would own their land and sell their goods at a fair market price. Through Jai Yu's efforts, Huangshan commune, which is a part of Li-ching village, became an early adopter of private land ownership in China.

In the first democratic election for village chief, Jai Yu won and immediately set to work on improving agricultural yields. Jai Yu refused to allow another child to endure the scorching pain of hunger.

Today, although he is retired, it is correct to address him as General Secretary He, as Jai Yu held that position for more than a decade. Jai Yu listened to the people in his village and took both their complaints and their suggestions to heart. He improved things so much that he became General Secretary over several townships.

"I am very happy," he says. "Yes, I am very happy. I have always been happy. I choose to be happy."

Jai Yu offers these three suggestions for becoming happier.

1. **Be confident:** Hold a vision of something you want, and then work to consciously expect that it will be yours. "If you can believe it, you can achieve it," Jai Yu says. "I wanted to become the leader of the village, but when I first shared that thought, people scoffed. But I maintained my vision."

   The more confident you feel, the happier you are.

2. **If there is a problem, communicate:** Every problem is, ultimately, a communication problem. If you are having a problem, consider how you might communicate better. "When I

see a problem," Jai Yu says, "I do everything I can to generate communication."

3. **Don't act your age:** "Hang around younger people," Jai Yu suggests. Do things that are fun and youthful. And part of being youthful is exercising. Jai Yu plays basketball with much younger men every day. He also rides his bike and plays table tennis daily.

"People today starve for happiness the same way we starved for food," Jai Yu says with great compassion. "However, no one can skim off the top of your happiness unless you let them."

With a laugh he adds, "Don't let them."

THE LANGUAGE OF HAPPINESS

In Chinese, the *fu* character symbolizes the word *happiness. Fu* means "good fortune" as well.

A MOTHER'S HAPPINESS

A woman discovers that the thirst-quenching happiness of motherhood can flow from many wells.

Being a mother is an attitude, not a biological relation.
—Robert A. Heinlein

You grow up, you marry the man of your dreams, and together you have a baby," Patti says, tossing her head back. The movement causes a golden lock of blonde hair to cascade over her shoulder.

Patti Stark owns a yoga studio in a small Midwestern town. She is of Scandinavian descent with fair skin, clear blue eyes, and fine blonde hair. And there is one more thing you should know about Patti—she giggles frequently.

Patti's giggling is not the nervous tic of someone who cannot bear pauses in conversation. Nor is it the submissive tittering of someone who has been cowered by life. Patti's giggling seems to be a release valve that prevents her glee from boiling over. She's *that* happy.

And she loves her husband, Steve.

"Steve and I were together for seven years before we got married," Patti says, smiling warmly. "Steve already had a daughter, Melissa, from a previous marriage. I loved her from the very beginning."

"Still," she continues, "after we finally got married, it felt like the next step was to have a baby. So, we began trying to get pregnant.

"And the trying was fun!" Patti says, her face flushing ever so slightly. "But, unfortunately, after a year of trying I still wasn't pregnant."

Doctors checked both Steve and Patti and found no medical reason for their inability to conceive. The couple opted to give artificial insemination a try. Patti was prescribed a fertility drug, and her hormone levels were artificially bumped up.

"It was crazy," says Patti. "I started getting hot flashes and all of my emotions intensified. If I was feeling insecure or sad because I wasn't getting pregnant; the artificial hormones intensified the feeling."

Patti's ramped-up hormones put a strain on her relationship with Steve. What was supposed to be a joyous experience—the conception of a child—was feeling more like a stressful science experiment.

"I was filled with fear, guilt, and sadness," Patti admits. "I felt insecure; my hormones were out of balance. I started to get migraines. I was a completely different person."

Holding up the five fingers of her right hand and wiggling them before her, Patti adds, "We tried artificial insemination five times." Then, bringing her index and thumb together, she says, "Zero successes."

Patti's countenance becomes sour, an expression that seems foreign to her typically cheerful face. "So, next we went to an in vitro specialist."

"We sat in the in vitro doctor's office, and the first thing he said was, 'I'm going to give you a drug that will shut down your pituitary gland.'" Patti leans forward and whispers conspiratorially, "After that, I didn't hear a word he said. I just felt like, *I'm done. I'm through with this.*"

For months, Patti pushed aside her dream of becoming a mother. However, try as she did to let motherhood go, she could not find a way to release her innermost desire to be a mom, and the couple began to look into adopting a child.

"We looked into adopting here in the United States and were told it could take five to seven years for a healthy baby. Plus, in our state the birth mom has six months to rescind the adoption. So we started looking internationally."

As luck would have it, on February 13 of that year, Patti's birthday, a woman in a small Mayan village in Guatemala, a woman Patti had never met, was in the process of giving her and Steve the greatest gift a woman can give. She was giving her child up for adoption.

When they heard his story and saw his picture, Patti and Steve knew. They knew that the young Mayan boy, whom they planned to name David, was their son. For more than a year, their attorney visited Guatemala monthly, taking videos that showed how David was progressing.

Several times the couple was booked to fly to Guatemala to collect their son only to be thwarted by Guatemalan red tape.

"Nearly a year after David became available for adoption," Patti says excitedly, "we were finally able to go and get him. When we left home, there was ten inches of snow on the ground. When we arrived in Guatemala, it was a steamy ninety-five degrees."

Patti forgot the temperature change, forgot the hassles, forgot the frustrations and the red tape, forgot it all when she looked into David's coffee-colored eyes. As she held him tight and breathed him in, Patti felt complete for the first time since she and Steve had married.

Arriving home, Patti lost herself in the shift from trying to become a mother to trying to become a good mother. She soon found that there is a great deal of patience, effort, and love required to shepherd another soul through the shadowy early-dawn years of life.

When David turned five, both Patti and Steve learned that being his mom and dad was going to carry a lifetime of unique challenges. They had noticed that David was developing well below norms for his age. He didn't walk until he was twenty months old, which at first was attributed to it being common for Guatemalan children to be two before they start walking. But he also struggled with some basic motor skills and seemed well behind norms in mental development.

A doctor's diagnosis explained the cause: fetal alcohol syndrome.

Today, David has trouble being around groups of people, and he experiences great difficulty focusing his attention. His memory is poor, and he has a particular challenge working with numbers.

David has his struggles, but he never struggles with the question, "Am I loved?" Thanks to Patti and Steve, David knows the answer.

Mothers of all children can feel overworked and under-appreciated, and can struggle to be happy. Patti offers these three suggestions for being a happier mom (or dad).

1. **Be in the moment:** "Every time I look into David's eyes," Patti says, "I try to remind myself that his soul is supposed to be here in my life. In the times when he's being difficult or making a mess, I do my best to accept him where he is.

    "I don't know if he'll ever be able to count to one hundred someday. I don't know if he'll be able to drive a car or hold a job. But right now he's perfect just the way he is."

2. **First, be happy yourself:** Caring for a child can deplete you. Patti and Steve keep themselves happy as a couple by going on frequent dates. Additionally, they keep themselves happy as individuals by enjoying their favorite solo activities.

    "Steve still plays soccer every week, and I do yoga," Patti says. "We like to listen to live music and go dancing. We keep our lives happy and, therefore, we have happiness to share with David."

3. **Be grateful for what you get because what you get is always what's best in the long run.** Patti explains, "I believe with every fiber of my being that adopting a special needs Mayan child from Guatemala was better for me than having my own child. He has taught me so much."

    She places a loving arm around David's neck. David, now a wiry ten-year-old, leans in to snuggle with his mom as he smiles his charming, crooked little smile. Patti says gently, "I don't take things for granted. That is a gift from David. And for that I'm a happier person."

THE LANGUAGE OF HAPPINESS

In the Yucatec Maya language, the language of David's village, the phrase for happiness is *ki'imak ool* (key-mack-ool).

GIVING HAPPINESS

A college student discovers real happiness when he starts a company to help feed starving people.

You have not lived today until you have done something for someone who can never repay you.
—John Bunyan

Yo . . . Yo, dude, stop the car!" cried Bryan from the backseat.

"What? What's up?" asked the friend who was driving.

"*Stop* the car!" Bryan repeated.

"Yeah, man, pull over," said Andrew, who was sitting next to Bryan.

"Dudes . . . we're already late," droned another friend who sat in the passenger seat, head down, hood up, eyes focused on Angry Birds.

"It'll only take a sec," Bryan urged. "C'mon, man, pull over."

The car eased over to the curb and everyone hopped out. Together, they helped a driver push his stalled car out of a busy intersection. Having helped clear the car and then loaned the driver a cell phone so that he could call for help, the young men jogged back to their vehicle.

"That felt good," Bryan said. The other guys each injected some form of agreement.

For more than ten minutes, not a word was spoken. The driver pressed the accelerator, attempting to make up for lost time. He, like the rest, was smiling.

Andrew broke the silence: "It'd be cool to feel like that more often, ya know?"

"I was just thinking that," Bryan said. And he began to tell everyone about his friend who helped feed starving people in Nepal. "There are people in rural Nepal who are dying of starvation," he explained. "My friend's group buys this fortified peanut butter stuff and sends it there. It keeps people alive."

"Cool," Andrew said. "I'll bet he feels great all the time."

"You know . . ." Bryan's voice trailed off for a moment, then he continued, "we could, maybe, make some T-shirts and sell them and use the money to help buy fortified peanut butter for those starving people in Nepal."

"I'm in," Andrew said, not requiring any further convincing.

For the other guys, the experience had been interesting and possibly even significant. For Bryan, it was both pivotal and transformational.

Bryan Simpson, age twenty-five, still resides in his hometown of Springfield, Missouri. "We'd been on our way to a soccer match," he recalls. "That's all we did in those days—play soccer."

With a sly smile Bryan corrects himself, "Actually, we did three things: play soccer, go to class, and party.

"Our focus was on ourselves and what we wanted to do," Bryan confides. "We were self-absorbed. But that day when we helped that guy . . . man! I felt like I'd been given the key to happiness. I just wanted to find ways to give, to really give."

Bryan convinced his parents to purchase rudimentary screen printing equipment, which he and his best friend, Andrew Bordelon, set up in the living room of the Drury University Soccer House. The two of them watched how-to videos on YouTube to learn screen printing.

"We'd do some shirts for the team and we'd be really proud, but . . . wow, looking back on them now, they were pretty awful. We really had no idea what we were doing," he says.

Their craftsmanship may have been evolving, but their purpose was clear—*give*!

People would call to place orders, and Bryan would ask how the caller had heard of their little venture. He or she would typically respond: "Our company budget includes money for marketing and team-building items, such as T-shirts—but not for making the world better. We want you to print our T-shirts—not because you're the cheapest, but because we want to give back. And working with you really gives back."

Orders came in from more than one hundred miles away. Bryan was busy—very busy, but also happy—very happy. He was working for a law firm during the day, tending bar at night, going to class when he could, and printing shirts in between. More importantly, money was going to Nepal Nutrition.

Andrew left the venture six months in. He was enjoying it but had always wanted to become a soccer coach, and that desire pulled him back on track. Bryan found people willing to help out.

Then came the T-shirt order that almost killed the dream.

"Missouri State University offered us a contract—a really *big* contract—and so I went down and applied for a business license,"

Bryan says. "But when I told the woman at the business license bureau that we printed T-shirts in our living room, we were told that we were violating city code, and they shut us down. I found some space in an old, run-down historic building, but being kids, basically, with no collateral, the banks wouldn't talk to me."

Bryan pauses a moment to let the emotion in his voice clear. "My dad agreed to push his retirement back to help us keep going. We changed our whole business model, and we now not only do screen printing, but we have retail stores. For every T-shirt we sell for twenty dollars, five pounds of fortified peanut butter is sent to stop malnutrition. That's why we call our company Five Pound Apparel. But we didn't want to stop there, so we decided to carry other brands that also give back. So every sale made in our store gives back in some way."

In just its first couple of years, Five Pound Apparel has supplied the starving people of Nepal with 7,500 pounds of fortified peanut butter, the shoeless people of the third world with 1,200 pairs of shoes, and has raised $10,000 for local charities.

Impressive numbers. Bryan then adds one more number as if it were the least significant, "Sales are up 40 percent this year over last."

Bryan is still happy—*very happy*—and he offers three observations about happiness.

1. **Incorporate giving into your life:** "As soon as you do," says Bryan, "your problems become so much smaller. When you start working with people who are dying of malnutrition, whether your iPhone 4 is getting good reception begins to seem a lot less important."

2. **Live like you want to live.** "I'd rather travel the world than have a big home. If I can work forty rather than sixty hours a week and be happy, that's what I'll do. With a growing

company, it's always a battle *not* to work. But we travel, and I ride my bike a lot."

3. **Truly step back and figure out what makes you happy:** "I see all these kids my age taking jobs they hate to make $50K. It blows my mind that people are willing to take any job just for money. There is no way to substitute a salary for your passion in life."

Bryan has one last piece of advice, "Live simply," he says. "For a guy with a clothing store, I own fewer clothes than most people."

He looks down at his Five Pound Apparel T-shirt, shrugs, and adds, "Owning a bunch of stuff just weighs you down, you know? But helping people, man, that makes you happy!"

THE LANGUAGE OF HAPPINESS

In Nepali, "I am happy" is *sukha* (sook-ha).

KINDNESS = HAPPINESS

A mother and father demonstrate the link between kindness and happiness.

Those who are not looking for happiness are the most likely to find it, because those who are searching forget that the surest way to be happy is to seek happiness for others.
—Dr. Martin Luther King Jr.

To understand Steve Bedford, you need to know a little something about his parents.

A Story about Steve's Father, Bill

Reverend Bill Bedford sat impassively.

What appeared to be a smile on his face was actually a practiced expression. His gritted teeth were ensconced behind lips that curled upward at the ends in an effort to look pleased.

Bill wasn't pleased.

A man in a dark-blue suit sat directly across from Bill. The man was tall and rawboned with eyes nestled deep in his skull. His pockmarked cheeks made his face look like burlap.

"That gall-blasted Kennedy is running for president!" the man exclaimed. "And you know what he is, right?"

"A Catholic!" said the other three men packed tightly with them in Bill's small office. Two sat on either side of their speaker, while one paced nervously back and forth in front of the only window.

"Ex-actly!" the man said, pumping his wrinkled fist in the air. "And if he becomes president . . ."

"If he becomes president," the nervous man said, stopping his pacing and placing both hands on Bill's desk so as to face him squarely, "Kennedy will take his orders from the Pope."

"Catholicism will become the official religion of the United States." The man in the blue suit injected. "The Pope will be our leader. Kennedy will be his puppet. Our faith . . . *everything* will be gone."

Bill breathed deeply and maintained his "smile."

"You need to write a sermon," the man continued. "You need to write a sermon telling people not to vote for Kennedy!"

All four men stared at Bill, anxiously awaiting his next words.

"Gentleman," Bill said, rising and extending his right hand to indicate that the meeting was now over. "Thank you for sharing your concerns with me. Let me give this prayerful consideration."

Later, Bill sat on the porch, relating the incident to Steve, who was quite young. Steve asked, "What are you going to do, Dad?"

"As a minister, my role is to model kindness for others," Bill said. "Now, how kind would it be if I took potshots from the pulpit at a man whose only crime, as I can see it, is practicing a different religion than mine?"

A Story about Steve's Mother, Curtiss

Curtiss Bedford really didn't need to work. She just knew that if her life was comprised exclusively of hosting teas, leading the women's Bible study, and the other activities associated with being a minister's wife, she'd go crazy.

Curtiss got a job working for Meyers-Arnold department store. She worked down in the basement, selling clothing. Curtiss loved getting to meet and talk to a wide variety of people, and everybody in Greensboro shopped at Meyers-Arnold.

Curtiss frequently ate lunch at the Woolworth's across the street. When she showed up for lunch on Monday, February 1, 1960, the crowd of people standing around the lunch counter surprised her.

Four African American freshmen from North Carolina Agricultural and Technical College had sat down in four empty seats at the counter. The problem was that those empty seats were in the whites-only section.

"Excuse me, ma'am," one of the students said calmly and respectfully to an elderly waitress. "We're still waiting for our coffees."

The woman busied herself emptying ashtrays and wiping the counter. The store manager stood nearby, pretending to read a newspaper. A police officer swiveled his body toward the four men and began to tap loudly on the handle of his nightstick.

Curtiss surveyed the scene. Here were four young men; polite, well groomed, cordial, and they were being met with hostility.

Why should they have to sit apart from everyone else? she wondered.

Curtiss wasn't scheduled to work the following day, but she went to Woolworth's on the pretext of having lunch. To her surprise, the same four students had returned to sit at the lunch counter. This time, however, nineteen supporters joined them. The following day, eighty-five people showed up to lend their support to the men and their cause. By week's end, the number swelled to four hundred.

Doesn't the Bible say that we are to treat everyone as we would want to be treated? thought Curtiss.

The sit-in dragged on for several months.

Would I want to be forced to sit apart from other people because it isn't socially acceptable to be around people like me? No, she thought to herself, *no I wouldn't.*

"This isn't right," Curtiss told her family that night at dinner. "Those young men deserve the same treatment we would receive." Having made her stance clear to everyone at the table—all of whom agreed with her—Curtiss took another mouthful of food and chewed slowly.

The Bedford family was living at what would soon be the epicenter of an earthquake of civil rights controversy in America. The parents were being pulled to side with "people like them." However, Bill and Curtiss embraced everyone as being people "like them."

Bill and Curtiss taught their children the importance of kindness. They demonstrated with their own lives that caring for people means caring for and about *all* people.

Steve Bedford Today

When Steve's father died, it was very hard on Steve, but he is grateful to have had a father he loved so much that his passing proved so painful. Steve remains very close to his mother.

Steve is now sixty-four years old and is a very happy guy. He owes a lot of his happiness to the lessons he learned from his mom and dad. Here are three of those lessons to apply in the cultivation of your own happiness.

1. **Be kind.** When you are kind, the happiness you see on the other person's face is a reflection of how happy you feel doing something nice. Treating other people well is an affirmation of your connection to everyone.

   "*Be kind to people* was like a mantra my parents said to me," Steve says. "When you realize that everyone deserves your compassion and your kindness, and then you treat people that way, it just makes you feel happy."

2. **Be open:** "My dad was an ordained minister, and everyone expected him to have all the answers. But he didn't, and he freely admitted it. And, as a result, he learned a lot from other people. Learning keeps you growing and growing makes you feel happy."

3. **Be grateful:** Steve has a thirty-six-year-old son named Tim. Tim has Asperger's syndrome.

   "People look at Tim and ask me, 'What's wrong with him?' to which I always respond, 'Nothing. He's perfect just the way he is.'"

   Steve's face beams with contentment. "Be kind to everyone," he says again. "It's not about making them feel good—it's about making *you* feel good."

HAPPY ANYWAY

A woman stays happy even after several injuries that end her career and leave her with chronic pain.

What lies behind you and what lies in front of you, pales in comparison to what lies inside of you.
—Henry Stanley Haskins

C arol lay still in the predawn darkness. She had been awake for several minutes, but she hadn't stirred. Her husband, Matt, lay next to her, snoring softly.

Carol was awake. She didn't need any more sleep. She had things to do. And yet, she lay still.

As usual, Carol took a few moments to savor the combination of being both awake and being still. In that golden time after she awoke, but before she rose and went about her day, Carol rested in a state of blissful ignorance.

At this point, Carol didn't know. But soon she would.

Presently, Carol would move to get out of bed, and at that point she would know what level of pain she would be facing that morning. For Carol, her daily pain level was like a random weight handed to a runner just before a marathon. Some days the weight of Carol's pain was light, barely noticeable. Other days, it was a two-ton anvil crushing her and forcing her to stay immobile until it passed.

"Can versus can't—it's a choice," Carol said in a half whisper as she pushed herself up to a seated position. "Okay, world, here we go."

Carol walked slowly to the kitchen. While the coffee was brewing, she scooped up her handful of morning meds. Carol is used to the medications now. They help, but she doesn't rely on them.

"My day is up to me," Carol says. She sips a cup of coffee, stretches, and walks over to her art table to finish up some bookmarks she'd begun the night before.

Unyielding pain that includes severe migraines—this is Carol's life. And yet, according to those who know her best, Carol is a very happy person.

Carol Stevenson had enjoyed her job. Whenever someone asked what Carol did for a living, she took pride in her response. Often, the person being thus informed would respond with some variation of "Really?" or "That's cool."

Carol had been the director of operations for the local food bank. Through her efforts and those of a great many volunteers, tens of thousands of people ate every day.

"I got a call that there was a pallet of frozen food available." Carol says. "It was in the heat of summer and somebody had to get it quick before it spoiled. Besides, you don't want to turn down food. Not only is it wasteful, but the vendors who give you their donations might stop if you don't respond."

Carol couldn't find an available volunteer, so she went alone to pick up the food.

One by one Carol heaved the heavy boxes of frozen shrimp, fish, ice cream, berries, and other items into her station wagon. As she raised one case high to place it upon another, she felt a searing pain in her shoulder.

Carol waited a moment for the pain to pass and tried raising her arm. As soon as her arm reached a certain point, the pain returned with ferocity. Carol knew she had seriously injured herself.

Carol's rotator cuff was torn—a very painful and debilitating injury. Carol went to see a doctor who tried to manage her pain through mind-numbing narcotics rather than surgery to repair the problem.

Carol did her best to work, although she was relegated primarily to doing paperwork and managing others.

One day, a woman volunteered to take on some of the clerical tasks at the food bank. Carol was elated and began to prepare on office for her. As Carol moved some furniture around, she got her foot caught between a desk and a file cabinet. As she pulled to wrench her leg free, Carol both heard and felt something tear.

Now Carol had a seriously injured right shoulder and her right ankle was injured to match. Carol was given more medication. "I just felt dopey all the time," she says.

Because of her hobbled gait, Carol had trouble climbing stairs. Once, she was walking up a flight of stairs, carrying some copy paper when, because her right foot dragged somewhat behind her, Carol missed a step and began to fall.

"It was like being in slow motion," she says. "I started to fall forward and instinctively put my hands out to catch myself. *But*, as soon as my right hand touched the ground, I felt this indescribable pain in my shoulder."

Without even thinking, Carol twisted her body around 180 degrees and crashed down hard, striking her head and snapping her neck.

Carol doesn't know how long she was unconscious. When she awoke, she saw her boss's face and heard him advise her not to move.

That was the end. Carol had chronic bulging discs with pain and inflammation of the neck vertebrae just above her shoulders. She could no longer carry items for the food bank, she could no longer walk, and she could no longer even sit and work in the office. With great sadness, Carol applied for and, after many months, received full disability.

Now, whatever Carol does, wherever she goes, she carries some degree of pain with her. Her shoulder was finally repaired surgically, but she still has enduring difficulties with her ankle, and the injury to her neck has left her with myriad ailments.

"My attitude is the most important possession I have," Carol says passionately. "I can lie in bed doped up on pain meds and antidepressants, or I can find ways to enjoy my life. I choose the latter."

Carol designs and creates beautiful custom greeting cards and bookmarks to commemorate special occasions. In addition, she sells some of her more popular designs through bookstores and coffee shops.

"It's a way of feeling productive," she says, "and of augmenting my meager disability check."

Even while bearing the weight of chronic pain, Carol manages to keep an upbeat attitude and find ways to creatively contribute. She is happy. Here are Carol's three suggestions for how you can be happy too.

1. **Don't be a victim of your pain:** Everyone carries emotional or physical pain or both. To stew in anger and resentment over what someone has done to you only sacrifices the present to the specter of the past.

   Carol found that many of the pain medicines she was taking either made her depressed or caused her to become fuzzy-headed. She worked with her doctors to tone down her pain meds so that she could accept the responsibility of keeping her spirits up herself.

   "If pain is keeping you from doing what you want to do, in many ways that's a choice," Carol says. "I will always have pain, but I'm not going to sit and focus on it. I'm going to be productive."

2. **Find reasons to laugh—often:** Laughter causes endorphins—endogenous morphine, to be released into the body. When you laugh, you are doping yourself up with natural painkillers.

   Listen to comedy recordings, hang around funny people, and watch comedies on TV and at the theater.

   Carol has several girlfriends who share her offbeat sense of humor. When she needs a laughter pick-me-up, she'll call one of them and very soon she'll find herself laughing and feeling happier with her pain diminished.

   Find reasons to laugh, and as you do, your pain—be it physical or emotional—will diminish.

3. **Have a Girlz Gang (or Guyz Gang):** Carol has a group of women friends—about twenty or so—who get together approximately once a month. Many of them have chronic pain and other issues, but Girlz Gang get-togethers are not a time for the women to process their problems.

"No," Carol explains. "Girlz Gang get-togethers are where we can laugh, have fun, and tease. We want to take our minds off our problems, not focus on them."

Cultivate a gang of fun, upbeat people and get together with them regularly. There is not only strength in numbers, there is healing as well.

HAPPILY EVER AFTER

A woman's husband passes away, and she finds happiness comforting others who are experiencing grief.

If you would indeed behold the spirit of death, open your heart wide unto the body of life. For life and death are one, even as the river and the sea are one.
—Kahlil Gibran

What surprised Leal Roberts most was the force of the wind. Not the roar from the open door or the surreal view of the earth thirteen thousand feet below. No, it was the power of the wind whipping her body around as she prepared to jump.

Every time she tried to put her foot on the narrow step welded just beneath the door of the plane, the wind blew it off, leaving her scrambling. Finally, her instructor, who also happened to be functioning as her parachute, grabbed Leal's foot and pressed it to the step.

She was clamped to his chest via a system of hooks and straps. She was so much smaller than he was that Leal thought she must look like a baby in a Snugli.

"One . . ." said the instructor.

Leal noticed the videographer preparing to jump with them. She tried to remember instructions—not the ones related to the jump; she felt like she knew those. No, she wanted to remember the videographer's advice as to how to look her best for the camera.

"Two . . ."

"Smile, or else the skin on your face will be jiggling," he had advised her.

Leal pressed her lips back into a wide smile. She did *not* want to have a commemorative video that showed her with jiggling skin like an old woman. She was only fifty-eight and was by no means "old."

"Three!"

The instructor rolled his large body out the door, taking her much smaller body with him. Leal smiled a forced smile as the two of them stepped into nothingness.

I'm doing it! Leal thought. *I'm actually skydiving.*

A few weeks before, Leal had groaned when she read the hospice newsletter. Although she appreciated the hospice for all the support it had given her, the newsletter's suggestions for commemorating the anniversary of the death of a loved one struck Leal as boring.

Plant a tree, Leal read. *Take a walk in nature.* "Bor-ing," she said under her breath. "I'll bet Dick is bored by this stuff, and he's dead."

No. Leal wanted to do something more spectacular to celebrate the anniversary of Dick's passing. Inside the pocket of her lime-green jumpsuit was a baggie containing the last of his ashes—the rest having been spread in various locations around the world. For a year she had been carrying Dick around with her—both literally and emotionally—and she was ready to let him go.

Dick had been her best friend, her lover, her husband. She had known he had cancer before they got together and had nursed him when it resurfaced. She had loved and cared for him right up until the end.

After the jump, Leal grabbed the DVD of her skydive and walked triumphantly to her car. Somehow the experience had made her feel complete. Good friends had arranged a gathering of several people for that evening, and one of the invitees was a blind date for Leal.

"My friends convinced me to show the video of my jump from earlier that day," says Leal. "I was seated next to my date. When I got to the part in the video where I honored Dick, my date leaned over and clinked his wine glass to mine. That simple gesture let me know that he, too, was very special."

His name was Don. He was interesting, sweet, loving, and exciting. Leal was smitten, and the two began to date and spend time together.

Two and a half years into their relationship, Don, an avid golfer, fulfilled a longtime dream of playing the course at Pebble Beach, California. After playing eighteen holes, Don lay down on the beach to rest, while Leal jogged along the shore.

As Leal finished her run, she walked up to Don napping on the beach. Gently kicking his leg, she said playfully, "Hey buddy, there's no sleeping on the beach—you gotta move it."

Don didn't respond.

Leal's hands were cold from being licked by the cold wind while she ran. She leaned over and placed her cold fingers on Don's neck in an attempt to startle him. He didn't move.

"Oh no," she thought to herself. And then she cried, "Don! Don, can you hear me?"

The next hour was a blur. A blur of giving Don CPR until Leal was exhausted and then a young man took over for her. A blur of people stopped to gawk. She saw Don's face being covered for the last time and his body being rolled by EMTs to a waiting ambulance.

After her first husband, Dick, died, other recent widows contacted Leal to seek her consul and support for getting through the difficult and painful process of grief. Leal talked honestly and openly with these surviving lovers whose loves had preceded them in death.

Now these same women rallied around Leal to support her through her second major loss in just a few short years.

Leal was crushed, but she counted herself as having been lucky to share her love with two wonderful men. For a woman who has experienced having her life stripped bare of the men she loved, Leal is remarkably upbeat. She is very happy, and she loves life.

More importantly, she has found healing for herself by working to help other women heal.

Leal offers the women she counsels suggestions for how to move past the hurt and find happiness again. Her advice to them is applicable to anyone who wants to become happier.

1. **Get past your story:** "You are not you," Leal says. "You are the story you tell yourself. If you tell yourself that you are cursed or unlovable, then that's the story you get to live with."

For example, Leal doesn't describe herself as a widow.

"I'm a vibrant young woman out in the world," she says.

2. **Go through the process:** Grief is a progression and takes time to work through. "When I show up to counsel a woman who has lost her husband," Leal says, "I don't bring a Bible, I bring a bottle of wine. Together, we drink, we laugh, we cry, we share. We allow the pain to come to the surface so that we can let it go. Stifling what you're feeling is only going to make the pain endure."

3. **Learn to love yourself:** Leal observes, "Women are always looking for someone outside themselves to love them. You have to learn to love yourself. You don't need a man in your life to complete you; you are already complete."

    Some people feel anger and resentment toward a loved one who has died, but not Leal. "There's no way these two guys would have chosen to leave me," she says. "I'm way too much fun!"

HAPPY TO BE OF SERVICE

Hospice Foundation of America: www.HospiceFoundation.org

HAPPY TO BE OF SERVICE

In the midst of hate, one man shares happiness by planting a flag for love.

It is better to light a single candle than to curse the darkness.
—Chinese proverb

Aaron Jackson clicked "Send" on his smartphone. With that, the fuse was lit, and the clock was running.

After months of careful negotiation and planning, everything was in place. All the preparation had been done under absolute secrecy. All information shared with anyone outside the project was given on a need-to-know basis only.

It would go down today.

Everyone was ready. Aaron knew that the job had to be completed as quickly as possible to limit the chances of anyone stopping them. He also knew that people would be watching closely, and this added to both his excitement and his anxiety.

Aaron felt in his heart that he was doing something important, and yet he didn't know if the people in his neighborhood would approve or if they would ridicule and possibly even attack him.

Aaron sipped his coffee, the caffeine overshadowed by the adrenaline coursing through his body. He sat in a modest little home on a nondescript side street. Just moments before, a crew of painters had begun applying the first coat of paint to his new home. It was with the first strokes of their brushes that Aaron allowed himself a contented smile as he sent the text telling his reporter friend to go ahead and release the story.

The coordination of effort—the secrecy, the urgency—had all stemmed from the three most important words in real estate: *location, location, location.*

Aaron's house is located at the corner of Twelfth and Orleans in Topeka, Kansas, and it is directly across from the Westboro Baptist Church.

Yes, *that* Westboro Baptist Church. The one with its web address GodHatesFags.com proudly displayed on a large banner hanging from the church's street side exterior. The same Westboro Baptist Church with members who regularly picket funerals of American soldiers, yelling that US military personnel are being killed as God's wrath for America's tolerance of gay people.

Shirley Phelps-Roper is the daughter of Westboro's founder, Fred Phelps, and is spokesperson for the ministry. In response to the Sandy Hook Elementary tragedy in which twenty-six people—nearly all of them children—were killed, Shirley Phelps-Roper tweeted: "Praise to God for the glory of his work in executing his judgment."

Two years ago, Aaron had been surfing the web, and he came upon a story about Westboro Baptist Church. Intrigued, he read everything he could find about the world-famous anti-gay ministry.

Aaron launched Google Earth to view the church's compound, and when he did, an inspired thought landed in his mind as gently as a butterfly grasping the tender tips of a summer flower.

Zooming in to view a house near Westboro's front door, Aaron saw a sign that read For Sale.

He discovered that the particular house he'd seen had already been sold. However, he found another house with an even more visible location.

"My inspiration was to paint a gay pride flag prominently on a house that was highly visible and near the church," Aaron says. "If Westboro had any idea that I was planning this, it'd use its resources and influence to stop me. So this had to be a fast, covert operation."

Within thirty minutes of Aaron allowing two reporters to post their stories online, the Rainbow House became a huge worldwide media event. "An hour into it," Aaron says with a grin, "CNN, Fox News, ABC . . . they were all here." And under the watchful eye of the world, the house was completed as planned.

Publicly, the Westboro Baptist Church has welcomed its neighbors in the Rainbow House, and friendly gestures are exchanged whenever people from WBC encounter a friend or volunteer of the Rainbow House.

To create a gay pride rainbow house directly across the street from Westboro Baptist would have to be something close to a miracle, but Aaron deals in miracles.

Call to mind the image of a starving child in the third world and you'll likely envision a child with a swollen abdomen. It isn't hunger but rather parasitic intestinal worms that cause these children to have distended stomachs.

Even if food were plentiful, 90 percent of children in countries like Haiti would be struggling to eat enough to feed both themselves and the ravenous parasites growing within their young bodies. One of the first things to do to eliminate third world hunger is to cure people of this internal infestation.

And that's what Aaron did. In his mid- to late twenties, he raised money and awareness to fund the treatment of intestinal worms for fourteen million Haitian children. For this, CNN awarded him Hero of the Year. Aaron did all of this while simultaneously starting two orphanages that were also in Haiti. He accomplished everything through trips back and forth between the United States and Haiti while supporting himself and his causes working as a golf caddy earning minimum wage plus tips.

Aaron isn't gay. He doesn't have an ax to grind. He didn't turn the house into a one-story gay pride flag to incite a mob or escalate a fight. Aaron bought the house to save lives.

"The suicide rate among gay teens is heartbreaking," Aaron says.

"We are ideally situated," he states with a wave of his arms. "Whenever anyone takes a photo of Westboro Baptist, they're going to get a picture of the Rainbow House right next to it.

"So," Aaron continues, a tremor in his voice, "when teenagers start to figure out that they are gay and are being hounded by others, we want them to know that there—right there next to a place that is committed to hating them—is a place committed even more strongly to letting them know how very much they are loved."

Aaron finds joy in helping people. It gives him a rush. It's what gets him up in the morning and keeps him going throughout the day. Aaron effuses happiness.

Happy people attract others to their causes because other people want to be around a happy person's energy and support it. Aaron believes that happiness is something you can increase if you keep the following three things in mind.

1. **Appreciate what you have rather than long for something else:** Aaron says, "It's really amazing to sit in a village in Haiti. Children there have only a fifty percent chance of reaching age four due to tuberculosis and starvation. You're looking around while people are dying, and everyone has a smile on their face. Then you come back to this country where we're drowning in a sea of wealth, and everyone is frowning. Why? Because people in the United States are focused on more. They can't take a few minutes to slow down and enjoy, really enjoy, what they have."

2. **Your life situation doesn't dictate your level of happiness:** What you're going through first has to go through you—your mind, that is. When something happens, you decide if you will see it as a major irritant or a minor inconvenience. You can choose to see something as a catastrophic end or a challenging beginning.

   "I have seen people in dire situations singing all the while," Aaron says. "We tend to react to life rather than choose how we'll respond."

3. **Be selfish about giving:** "The more I work on giving love and putting out to the world, the more comes back. It's to the point where so much love can come back from giving that giving can be a selfish act.

"So, what's wrong with that?" Aaron asks with a broad smile and a shrug of his shoulders. "I get to travel around the world. I have met some of the most famous people on Earth—and some of the poorest—and people's lives are better. That makes me very happy."

THE LANGUAGE OF HAPPINESS

In Haitian Creole, the word for happy is *bònn* (bahn).

THE GRAPES OF HAPPINESS

A woman discovers a happy career when she follows her heart.

A Jug of Wine, a Loaf of Bread—and Thou
Beside me singing in the Wilderness—
Oh, Wilderness were Paradise enow!
—Omar Khayyám

"I saw grapes," says Colleen with a wistful smile.

Colleen Gerke, which rhymes with *turkey*, had been at lunch when her husband, Jason, called saying, "You've got to see this house—right away."

That was all she needed to hear. Wiping the salad dressing from the corner of her mouth, Colleen rose quickly and headed for her car. The couple had been looking at potential new homes for several weeks. Colleen tended to love and see the potential in every house, whereas Jason had been cautious and selective.

As Colleen turned her car up the long, straight gravel driveway, she saw the house directly ahead. A smile spread across her face. Although designed to look like a classic American farm-house, the beige home perched atop the hill was obviously quite new. It rose three stories into the Missouri sky and had an enor-mous porch that held the promise of endless summer evenings.

As Colleen eased the car forward, she swept her head slowly from left to right, surveying the scene. To her left was a row of trees, ahead of her lay the house, and to her right were rolling hills.

"It was like a blank canvas," Colleen says. "And for some rea-son—I really don't know why—I could see rows of grapes lining the driveway even though there weren't any. It just seemed, well, right."

Everything had started when Jason's company held a corpo-rate outing in Weston, Missouri, a quaint little town just north of Kansas City. "It was a crisp fall evening," Colleen says. "Both Jason and I had grown up in the country and now worked for a major agricultural business. But our offices and home were in the city—we both needed more space."

Her eyes take on a dreamy quality. "That night under the sky, when we could really see the stars again, it was magical. We decided to find a new home near Weston. It would only be a forty-five-minute commute and well worth it."

Now, as Colleen arrived at the house just off Jowler Creek Road, it seemed like those very stars had aligned to bring them the perfect house.

An offer was made, there were some brief negotiations, and then the Gerkes closed on and moved into their new home—their wonderful, peaceful, serene home nestled amid sixteen acres of dark, rich land.

Once they had moved in and settled, the couple began to engage in one of their favorite hobbies—wine making. Colleen had taken a wine-making class in college. "I needed a class," she says, "and it was either chemistry or wine making.

"Now, I'm a twenty-year-old college student," she says, putting her two hands out like the bowls of an apothecary scale. "Chemistry," she adds with a scowl, lowering her left hand about an inch, "or a class where I get *free alcohol plus college credit*." Colleen smiles cheerfully and lowers her right hand nearly a foot, showing how easily the decision had been made.

"That first year in the house, we made wine in our basement—as usual," Colleen recalls with a smile, "Jason and I *love* making wine together. It's a wonderful experience.

"We love making wine together," Colleen repeats, "but growing the grapes . . ." Her voice takes on a sacred quality. "Growing the grapes is something we really enjoy."

For Colleen and Jason, working in the vineyard to grow the grapes is magical. In the evenings after work and all day on weekends, they would go together into the vineyard to tend their emerging crop.

Sometimes they would listen to music or talk. But more often than not they would work in silence, sensing the other person's closeness, savoring the thrill of sharing a common passion. As they heard only the wind and the music of chirping birds, Colleen and Jason watched their daily effort turn into a bountiful crop.

"It's so relaxing," Colleen says. "Grapevines are like little kids. They go where you train them to go, so you are always twisting them and combing them. It's wonderful to see a stick you plant turn into a sprawling canopy of vines heavy with grapes."

The original half acre planting of grapes became two acres, then five, and finally seven. The Gerkes were forced to make a decision. Either sell their beloved grapes to other winemakers, hoping the buyers would give their wine the same love Colleen and Jason had provided, or expand and become a winery themselves.

"We were fearless—we didn't know any better," Colleen says with a laugh. "We just started carrying bottles of wine to wine and grocery stores during our lunch hour. We'd put on a wine-tasting event and take orders. I doubt our customers knew we were making the wine in our basement."

Next, something surprising occurred—people began to show up at their home on the weekend. "Is this the winery?" People would ask after knocking on the Gerkes's door.

Colleen and Jason politely explained to visitor after visitor that, yes, they were indeed a winery, but they didn't have a facility that anyone could tour.

"People would show up and we'd greet them, then parade them through the house and down into the basement for wine tasting," Colleen says, laughing at the memory.

Colleen had been pregnant during their first harvest. She was pregnant a second time when she began to seriously consider making wine full-time. "It just all seemed so scary," she said. "I wanted a sign to let me know that I was going to be okay if I did this."

As fate would have it, Colleen's company reorganized and needed to cut staff. It offered a year's severance pay to anyone who was willing to resign. This was the sign Colleen had been waiting for.

Colleen and Jason built a new facility and now regularly host tours and other events at Jowler Creek Winery. From its meager beginnings nine years ago, Jowler Creek has grown to produce two thousand cases of wine in 2012.

More important than their success, Jason and Colleen are happy. They are doing work they love in a place they love—and they are doing it together.

Colleen recommends three things for becoming happy.

1. **Figure out what makes you happy:** People can become desensitized to their own feelings and emotions, and this makes it difficult to discern what brings them happiness.

    Ask yourself:
    -   What would you do all day if you could?
    -   What hobby or activity do you think about frequently?
    -   What magazine or news articles draw your attention?

2. **Do it every day:** Once you have figured out what brings you joy, do something related to it every day. Read an article on the Internet, call an expert, watch a video on YouTube, check Twitter feeds and Facebook fan pages, see if there are relevant LinkedIn groups.

    The secret to success at anything has always been and will always be:
    -   Consistency
    -   Time
    -   Consistency over time. Do a little something related to your passion every day and soon you'll find yourself becoming an expert at something you love.

3. **Experiment and have fun:** Keep your hobby, your job, even your marriage fresh by trying new things. And make having fun your highest priority in whatever you endeavor.

HAPPY NEWS

Research by Dr. Boris Hansel, of Public Assistance Hospitals, Paris, found that people who consume moderate amounts of wine tend to be less stressed and happier overall.

TRANSITIONING TO HAPPINESS

A woman finds happiness even after the greatest loss of all.

If we are mindful of the true nature of reality, then we never truly lose anyone—even to death.
—Thich Nhat Hanh

S anya was lying to her best friend.

She pretended not to know much—but she knew. She knew everything. And soon her best friend Angelia would know, as well.

Angelia and Sanya were conversing via cell phone as they both drove feverishly from opposite ends of town to meet at the hospital.

Angelia Ham had been working at a teen camp sponsored by the college that employed her. Her phone had rung a little after 1:00 a.m. It was Eric, her husband, calling to say that their eldest son, Kenny, had been hospitalized. Groggy from sleep, Angelia heard only one thing: "You'd better come."

Angelia immediately called Sanya to rally her support and was surprised to find her sounding fully awake. Sanya agreed to meet Angelia at the hospital.

Angelia rushed along the dark road. Sanya knew that there was no need to rush.

The two women met under the harsh lights of the hospital parking lot and managed a one-armed hug while walking briskly toward the emergency room.

"It *must* be serious," Angelia said gravely. "It's just not like Eric to call me if it's not."

Sanya was numb. It had been she—not Angelia—who had received Eric's first call. Eric knew that Angelia was going to need Sanya for what lay ahead.

As the women hurriedly stepped into the small emergency room in the small hospital that served their small town, Angelia was surprised at how quiet everything was. She was expecting there to be a buzz of activity. However, everything was as quiet as a tomb.

Angelia glanced about and saw her minister who, seeing Angelia, rose slowly. Despite his wrinkled brow, his face was gilded with warmth and what appeared to be a trace of sympathy.

Angelia turned and looked quizzically into Sanya's eyes— eyes that no longer had to filter out truth to bolster a charade.

The minister grasped one of Angelia's hands and Sanya wrapped both her hands around the other as they walked Angelia, dumbstruck with terror, through the large double doors.

When they arrived at the room, Eric's eyes were red and swollen. His body looked weak, insubstantial, as if Angelia could walk right through him.

Angelia saw Kenny lying motionless. She touched his arm, the arm that she, with her very life, had infused with warmth; it was now cold as stone. Her own arms flailed wildly for Eric as she dropped to her knees and wailed, "No! No! No!"

Kenny had been fourteen. He and his best friend, Gage, had been walking when Kenny complained of not feeling well. A second later, he was on the ground. Gage ran to get help, and Kenny's father was on the scene within minutes giving his son CPR.

But it was too late. For quite a while, Kenny had lived with a ticking time bomb nestled in his chest. Arrhythmogenic right ventricular dysplasia (ARVD) is a rare disease that causes the right side of the heart to become less and less productive over time. ARVD is difficult to diagnose and, as was the case with Kenny, is often fatal.

No one, not even Kenny, had any inkling that his heart could cease to function at any time and without warning.

Over the next four hours, Angelia and Eric talked, cried, prayed, talked some more, and cried a lot more. They gave thanks for Kenny's life, brief though it was, and they struggled with what they'd tell his sister, Kya, age six. They struggled even more with what they'd tell Kenny's brother, Eli. Eli was age four, ten years younger than Kenny, and he worshipped his brother. Both children were waiting at home with their grandmother.

Around 6:00 a.m., as the birds chirped their daybreak song and shook away the last drops of the previous night's rain, everyone departed for their homes.

They each walked slowly to their cars when one by one they looked up and were stopped mid-step by appreciative awe. There, painted across the horizon in radiant brilliance, was a stunning and quite perfect double rainbow.

The following week was a blur of endless decisions and details. There were myriad supportive offers and endless painful reminders. Life no longer seemed real.

A week to the day after Kenny died, the family needed to get away. They booked a hotel room in a nearby city and occupied themselves with sightseeing. Toward the end of the day, a dark cloud settled over Angelia and she began to cry.

Ever the nurturer, Kya had grown accustomed to her mommy's tears but never ceased her efforts to lessen them. As she hugged Angelia tightly, Kya looked out the window and then shouted, "Look, Mom!"

Angelia turned and was joined by Eric and Eli as the family stood in stunned silence, staring at a flawless double rainbow framed by their hotel room window.

Ever since Kenny had died, rainbows have appeared at just the right time to bring comfort to the family. "We say that Kenny has the rainbow remote," says Angelia. "We'll be facing a tough day and, boom, there's a rainbow. It's like Kenny is saying, 'I'm OK and so are you, and we'll be together again soon.'"

Experiencing the death of a child can be devastating. And yet, Angelia is considered to be a happy person, and she agrees with this assessment.

Whether you have known the pain of losing a child, you can benefit from Angelia's suggestions for happiness.

1. **Look for "God nods."** One night, not long after Kenny's death, the Ham's front doorbell rang. Angelia opened the door to find no one there. In their yard lay what appeared to be the remnants of a childish prank.

   Someone had strewn toilet paper across the Ham's front yard.

As Angelia walked into the yard, she could see that it wasn't a prank but, rather, a memorial. From behind the trees Angelia could hear giggling as she realized that the toilet paper actually spelled out k-e-n-n-y. Kenny's young friends had carefully spelled Kenny's name, securing the toilet paper to the ground with plastic forks.

This, according to Angelia, is an example of a God nod. A God nod is anything that lets you know you are loved and supported and are going to be okay.

2. **Realize that most of what bothers you really doesn't matter:** "Loss teaches you to appreciate everything," Angelia says. "So many things that drive you nuts are insignificant.

   "After Kenny died, I would just lie with Kya and Eli for hours. Thanks to Kenny, I'm now intentional about the time I spend with people. You don't know if this could be the last time you talk to someone, so treat your time with that person as if it were.

   "People," she says with a smile, "*that's* what matters."

3. **Sometimes you have to just live with it:** "People ask me how I got over Kenny's death, and I always say, 'I haven't.' You never get over something as tragic as losing a child. If you're going to survive, you have to let go of the life you once had—you have to establish a new normal. You have to accept what has happened, or you'll never be happy."

HAPPY TO BE OF SERVICE

Angelia and her family benefitted greatly from working with the Lost and Found Grief Center: www.LostandFoundOzarks.com

HAPPY VAGABOND

The new kid in town faces her fears by hitting the road.

I travel not to go anywhere, but to go. I travel for travel's sake. The great affair is to move.
—Robert Louis Stevenson

The air was filled with the sound of tennis shoes racing up and down slick marble. Their squeaks could be heard even above the din of excited preadolescent voices.

Dee had never heard so much noise before. She clutched her books tightly to her chest and walked, head down, staring at the floor beneath her feet. Occasionally she glanced up, attempting to read the teachers' names printed in all capital letters on small signs attached to the heavy oak doors.

Welcome to seventh grade in the big city, Dee thought to herself.

"Mrs. Allison . . . Mrs. Allison," Dee repeated under her breath. Amid the buzz of activity, she found comfort in keeping her gaze on the unmoving floor as she recited her teacher's name like a mantra.

Rounding a corner, Dee lifted her head and craned her neck to peer around two boys who stood laughing and pushing each other back and forth in front of one of the classroom doors.

For the first time in her life, Dee felt small. The average height of an American twelve-year-old girl is five foot four. Dee was four foot three. Dee is diminutive—she is pixieish. Dee is cute, and a large part of that cuteness comes from her size.

At that moment, Dee's petite stature wasn't adding to her cuteness, it was adding to her frustration. As she explored, it seemed like a taller student was forever positioned between her and every one of the classroom name signs.

Dee's family had spent the first twelve years of her life in Lewis, Kansas. In all of her years in school, it had been her and fifteen others. The same kids year after year, nine boys and six girls.

No one ever transferred into Dee's class. No one ever transferred out—until Dee.

Dee didn't know a single one of her new classmates. And there were *a lot* of new classmates. Dee had never imagined that there existed this many kids her own age in an entire city, much less all in the same school.

The irony is that her new home of Liberal, Kansas, was not a huge city, consisting of only about sixteen thousand citizens. However, perspective is reality, and to Dee the move from Lewis to Liberal may have well been a move to Tokyo. Dee felt that small, that lost, that insignificant.

"Mr. Clayton . . . Mrs. Schull . . . Mr. Oberndorfer . . ." Dee read the names printed on the doors she passed, hoping she would find her classroom before the bell rang.

Dee wondered two things: In a school that seems enormous, why is it that no one offers to help the new kid? How do all the other kids know that she is the new kid and manage to ignore her completely?

Dee had attempted to befriend several girls, but found their cliques impenetrable. Dee would catch the other girls laughing at her expense. She became the butt of jokes and teasing. Dee discovered the truth that no tongue is so cutting as that of a preteen girl.

Dee approached a classmate who happened to be a neighbor, and the two made a date to play together. The other girl stood Dee up.

"Not once," Dee says. "She stood me up four times."

Dee Maack is now sixty-one and still pixieish. Dee has a face that glows so brightly that speaking to her in person can give you the sensation of being caught in a tractor beam of happiness. So much happy energy pours forth from her that when you are conversing with her, you feel yourself becoming happier through osmosis.

"When that little girl—I can't even remember her name, didn't show up to play with me all those times," Dee says, "it spun my life in a whole different direction."

Dee titters happily, "I launched into a phase of self-discovery. I was in a new town and no one knew me. I could try on any persona until I found the one that suited me.

"I tried being the nerd, the dedicated student, the athlete . . . even the high school bitch," Dee says, slapping her knee. She laughs loudly admitting, "I wasn't a very good bitch."

Dee finally discovered the persona that fit her best. It was the one that had gotten her through the formative years in Lewis and the expansive years in Liberal: "I'm happy. I've always been happy—*that* is who I am. I'm the happy person."

It took Dee several years to fully acclimate to life in a bigger town, but the experience of this adjustment laid out a path for growth that intrigued her. What if rather than avoiding being the new person in a town, she actually adopted this as a lifestyle?

Dee chose nursing as a career because it seemed to be a field that was chronically understaffed and where one could earn a good living helping other people and still live a nomadic lifestyle.

Dee graduated nursing school at age twenty-two. She packed everything she owned, and as an unseasonable blizzard raged around her, she drove her Volkswagen Beetle from Wichita, Kansas, to Taos, New Mexico.

In Taos, she met and saw things she never knew existed— certainly not in Kansas. She met gays and lesbians, people who lived in communes, and people of every diverse color of the rainbow.

After a year in Taos, Dee put a large map of the western United States on her wall. She closed her eyes, waved her arms a bit, and spun around a few times. She then touched her finger to the map. In a few days Dee was on her way to her next home, Lander, Wyoming.

Another year passed, and the map went up again. After a similar ritual to the one just twelve months prior, Dee's small index finger pointed to Prescott, Arizona. Dee moved there.

Around that time, nursing agencies began to sprout up around the country. These companies place qualified nurses in jobs for varying lengths of time in different cities. Dee was *thrilled* when she heard of this and immediately signed on with an agency.

Dee, who had been by her account traumatized by being the new kid in the seventh grade, spent her adult years intentionally being the new kid as often as possible. She lived in dozens of cities and enjoyed the experiences each provided.

Dee offers these three suggestions for becoming happier.

1. **Be around happy people:** Look for people who are happy and spend time with them.

    Dee laughs. "This is easy for me because I'm so happy that unhappy people don't even want to be around me. I annoy them."

2. **Don't say anything you don't want to be true:** "Don't complain about things," Dee advises. "Complaining gives your problems energy and makes them last longer. Plus, it makes you feel bad."

3. **Dare to be the new kid:** Happy people tend to try and do new things frequently. "It's never too late to try something new," Dee says, "and you might just find something you like very much."

At age fifty-two, Dee finally shelved her wanderlust. After all those cities and all those new people, one very special person had managed to get Dee to stand still and grow roots. Dee met and fell in love with Bob.

As you look into Bob's face, you see the same happiness that shines forth from Dee. But you have to wonder if Bob is as happy as he seems or if he reflects Dee's happiness just as the moon reflects the light of the sun.

Either way, the two of them are very happy.

INHERITING HAPPINESS

A mother chooses a risky course of action to help her unborn baby.

If I have done anything in life worth attention, I feel sure that I inherited the disposition from my mother.
—Booker T. Washington

Jenny slowly closed the lid of her laptop. She closed the lids of her tired eyes at the same time. She drew long, slow, deep breaths trying to relax. It had been another late night doing research. Jenny slid the computer off the bed and placed it on the floor.

Jenny Harless is classically pretty. With bright blue eyes, high cheekbones, and an upturned nose, she looks like a Madame Alexander doll. Jenny's smile burns bright with happiness.

Jenny has a slight build—typically. At this point, her body seems to be growing a little more each day with her second child.

After Jenny closed the laptop, she draped an arm over her husband, Kevin, who slept silently next to her. As she faced another night of fitful sleep, Jenny reflected on the emotional roller coaster that had become her life.

First, Jenny's heart had soared when she found out that she was pregnant. Kevin would soon have a son with whom to play sports and four-year-old Hanna would have a baby brother.

Then Jenny's spirits crashed when doctors discovered that her pregnancy was ectopic, meaning that the baby was growing outside of her uterus. An ectopic pregnancy is fatal for the child and potentially fatal for the mother.

To protect Jenny's health, a diagnostic and curative (D&C) procedure was scheduled. A D&C is an invasive technique that, among other things, typically terminates a pregnancy. As the doctors worked on Jenny, they made a surprising discovery. The diagnosis had been incorrect—her baby was *not* developing outside of her uterus after all.

The D&C was immediately halted and everyone prayed that Jenny would not miscarry.

As the weeks passed and no problems arose, Jenny began to feel hopeful again—even excited. Her pregnancy was progressing smoothly. However, during a routine ultrasound, the nurse made a discovery that unnerved her.

"What?" Jenny asked, sensing something was amiss. Kevin arose from his seat to get a better view of the monitor.

A long, uncomfortable silence unraveled after which the nurse donned a façade of cheerful professionalism. Rising and smiling a little too broadly, she said, "I'll be right back."

Jenny lay on the examination table—waves of worry broke over her heart. Kevin held her hand. Neither of them spoke.

Finally, after what seemed like days, the nurse returned with her eyes downcast followed by Jenny's doctor. The doctor flashed a cardboard smile. Grasping the wand of the ultrasound device, the doctor made a few slow passes over Jenny's stomach. His face grew grim.

"There is an anomaly with the baby's spine . . ." The doctor's voice trailed off.

Jenny and Kevin's hearts began to thunder in their chests.

"We're going to have to look into this some more," the doctor said, downplaying the significance of the discovery. He printed a picture of the ultrasound for Jenny and Kevin that showed their baby, but not its back. Then, after instructing Jenny to return in a week, the doctor departed quickly.

For the next seven days, Jenny and Kevin scoured the Internet for information about spinal disorders in fetuses, infants, and newborns. They read a lot about spina bifida and other diseases of the spine. In the end, the couple sincerely wished that they had not delved so deeply because what they learned frightened them.

Spina bifida is caused when a mother receives inadequate folic acid during the months prior to or just after conception. Abnormalities in vertebrae create a bulge in the fetus's back that swells as the spine begins to grow outside of the body.

Children with spina bifida can be born with leg weakness, paralysis, clubfoot, bladder- and bowel-control problems, pressure sores, and abnormal eye movement, along with other physical and mental challenges.

Approximately one in one thousand babies contract the most serious type of spina bifida. Jenny and Kevin sat breathless as the doctor confirmed that their baby boy, whom they intended to name Nolan, had this most severe type.

The couple sat frozen in time as the doctor explained disabilities that Nolan might have. He even touched ever so lightly on the challenges of what they could expect in caring for their son his entire life.

Jenny and Kevin saw—in the inflated horror of their mind's eye—their baby's stroller evolving into a wheelchair and the feedings and changings continuing forever.

Jenny stared with disbelief into the doctor's eyes.

Kevin cleared his throat and grasped for a strand of hope. "What about intrauterine surgery?" Kevin asked. He had read online about the controversial new procedure in which a baby with spina bifida is operated on while still in the relative safety of its mother's womb.

"Too risky," the doctor said, dismissing the idea with a wave of his hand. "No, I'm afraid that's not an option—besides, insurance won't cover it."

Over the next several months, Jenny researched this new procedure for treating spina bifida in utero. The surgery had been performed eleven times over the previous four years, and the success rate was impressive.

Friends and colleagues raised $5,000 through golf outings, car washes, and bake sales so that the Harless family could make the first of three payments on the surgery totaling $15,000.

When Jenny applied for the intrauterine surgery, they were denied because their doctors thought that the procedure was too risky. The couple persisted and were told Jenny could have the surgery but only if they went through several weeks of preparation.

Preparation included spending full eight-hour days for several weeks with doctors who opposed the procedure vehemently, even though they had no firsthand experience with it. And because spontaneous labor was the most commonly feared side effect for intrauterine surgery, Jenny had to sit for several days with babies on a preemie ward at the hospital.

During the preparation phase, Jenny would go home each night and cry. She would then scour the Internet until well after midnight, searching for answers to her ever-growing list of questions and concerns.

Ultimately, Jenny had the surgery, and the long-term impact of spina bifida upon Nolan has been minimal—far less than would be typical for a boy born with the highest level of the disease.

Nolan inherited his mother's blue eyes and broad smile. More than anything, Nolan is grateful to have inherited Jenny's propensity for happiness. Jenny reminds us that happiness is a choice and offers three suggestions for becoming happier.

1. **Acknowledge your power:** When Nolan was born, Jenny fretted over how to parent a child with special needs. A wise nurse advised, "You decide whether he grows up crippled. Raise him like a cripple, and he'll be crippled. But raise him like a man who can do anything he sets his mind to, and he'll make you proud."

    "Wow," Jenny says. "When she said that, I realized how much of a role I would play in how Nolan would progress." From that moment forward, the family ceased to discuss Nolan's disease. Instead, they focused on what Nolan was capable of doing rather than the few things that were a challenge for him.

    Thanks to Jenny and Kevin's faith in Nolan, he has become even more accomplished than they'd hoped.

2. **Remember that you are here for a reason:** If you believe there is a purpose for being who you are, where you are, right here, right now, then life will have meaning and happiness.

   "Remember that you are here for a reason," Jenny repeats like a mantra to both Nolan and Hanna.

   Nolan's reason for being may be his desire to become the next hi-tech tycoon à la Steve Jobs or Bill Gates. And he's well on his way, already having created a program for computer games that has been downloaded more than thirty thousand times.

3. **Stay true to what you believe in:** Although the surgery had a good track record, *experts* repeatedly insisted that Jenny would not be helping her son by having the procedure, rather she would risk irreparably harming him.

   Jenny heard everyone out, and in the end she trusted her heart and went forward. And, as she looks up at Nolan now, tall and muscular with strawberry blond hair, she's very glad she did.

HAPPY TO BE OF SERVICE
www.SpinaBifidaAssociation.org

STRONG IN HAPPINESS

A man's life continues along happily even when ravaged by a fatal illness.

Fans, for the past two weeks you have been reading about the bad break I got. Yet today I consider myself the luckiest man on the face of the earth.

—Lou Gehrig

R ats!" David grumbled. Then he wondered, *Now what do I do?*

David Grace was standing on a ladder attached to the inside of a grain silo. The silo was just less than forty feet tall, and David was about halfway up. As a millwright, David's job was to help build these giant, cylindrical metal containers. It is physical work that requires precision and stamina because millwrights like David have to climb up and down the inner and outer walls of these structures many times each day.

David loved the physical exertion of his job, but over the last few months, his satisfaction in his work was slowly being replaced by a concern for his health.

It was this concern that created the dilemma in which he now found himself. David saw a nut attached to a metal bolt that seemed loose. It should be a simple matter for him to hold the ladder with one hand, reach down with the other, grab his wrench, and tighten the bolt. The problem was that David was nearly three stories up and would have to hold onto the ladder with his left hand while reaching down and grabbing the wrench with his right. Lately, David was having problems with his left hand.

He had noticed it about four months ago when he bent to pick up two heavy steel pipes. David grabbed them, one in each hand, but found that when he stood, his left hand couldn't grip tightly enough for him to lift the pipe.

A few days later, he lifted the same two pipes the same way and did so with no difficulty. David forgot about the weakness in his left hand until it happened again. This time, he couldn't lift a generator. A few weeks later, it happened again, and then again two days after that.

Since that time, David's left hand would occasionally and without warning lose its strength. Now, David found himself midway up a forty-foot ladder, and to do his job he would have to hold onto a rung with his left hand while he reached for the wrench in a pocket of his leather tool belt.

Climbing up and down the ladder had begun to concern David, but he knew that if his left hand ever failed him while climbing, he could snag the ladder quickly with his right. Now he was placing his safety and possibly his life into his own hands— specifically into the erratic grip of his left hand.

David took a deep breath and slowly lifted the fingers of his right hand away from the ladder as he simultaneously did his best to tighten the fingers of his left. David reached for the wrench with his right hand and tightened the bolt. Then, with a grateful sigh, he placed his right hand back on the ladder, slid the wrench back into its pouch with his left hand, and then carefully, very carefully, continued his climb upward, inspecting the enormous tube.

David had been to see a doctor who diagnosed him as having a pulled muscle in his forearm. He had explained to the harried doctor that his forearm didn't hurt but was just intermittently losing strength; the doctor shoved a prescription for muscle relaxers into David's hand and walked out. David threw the script into a trash can.

Another doctor diagnosed David as having panic attacks and prescribed accordingly. This prescription, too, found its way into the trash.

David went to yet another doctor. This one, unlike the others, actually examined him. He had David attempt various dexterity and balance tasks such as walking heel to toe and standing on one leg.

This doctor diagnosed David as having some form of neuropathy, meaning that David had an unspecified disease of his peripheral nerves. By this point, David was finding other muscles in his body that were beginning to show sporadic weakness.

Finally, he was referred to a neuropathy specialist, and after five days of tests and several anxious weeks of waiting, the doctor gave David his report.

"You have ALS—also known as Lou Gehrig's disease," the doctor said. Amyotrophic lateral sclerosis (ALS) is a progressive neurodegenerative disease that affects nerve cells in the brain and the spinal cord. One by one, muscles cease to function until the patient's body can no longer sustain itself.

ALS is fatal. Typically, ALS patients die when their diaphragms no longer have the strength for them to inhale. Over days or even months, the person's breaths become increasingly shallow until he or she dies from asphyxiation.

It is an agonizingly slow and terrifying way to die.

The average life span for an ALS patient is three to five years after diagnosis. And it has now been two years since David's diagnosis. He's thirty-nine years old.

David lives in a small nursing home. Friends and family visit often, and if they are asked, they will tell you that they visit David to get *their* spirits lifted rather than the other way around.

One of David's friends puts her reason for visiting David this way, "I just simply love David's outlook—he's always encouraging others. It's amazing. David heals me in ways I'm not sure he even knows."

Another friend says, "David was physically the strongest man I've ever known. Now, when he is no longer physically able to do things for himself, I see he's even stronger than I thought. David has strength where it belongs—inside. Whenever I come to visit him, *I* leave more encouraged."

In just a couple of years, David has lost nearly all ability to care for himself. One by one his muscles have failed until, at last, they gave themselves over to atrophy.

It's as if David's body is a house and Life is going from room to room, shutting off lights long before he is ready to leave. And yet all of us must leave at some point. David's departure is likely sooner than most—and certainly sooner than he or those who love him would like it to be.

Even as David's muscles diminish, his optimism and enthusiasm continue to soar ever higher. David offers three suggestions for being happy.

1. **Be kind:** Being kind not only makes you feel good, it can also make your life better. "The staff members here at the nursing home are wonderful people," David says, "but they *are* people. I have found that the nicer the patient is, the better care that person receives.

   "Oh, I don't think the nurses and aids actually treat grouchy people with less care on purpose. But it's human nature to want to give yourself fully to people you like, and being kind makes people like you."

2. **Look for something positive:** Happy people are also optimistic people. It is simply not possible to be a negative person and be happy.

   "I'm an optimistic person," says David. "So far, I have lost my ability to feed and clothe myself. I can't go to the bathroom without help—I can't even scratch when I itch. But I can still breathe, I can still swallow, I can still speak, I can still get on the computer. I know I'm going to lose the capacity to do these things, too, but I'm going to enjoy them while they last."

3. **Love:** "There are so many things and so many people in the world to love," David says. "Put your focus on those things— don't pay any attention to anything else. Learn to love where you are in life. Then, however long or short it may be for you, your life will be a happy and wondrous experience."

HAPPY TO BE OF SERVICE
Visit the ALS Association online at www.ALSA.org

RIVERS OF
HAPPINESS

A woman travels happily up the river of life well into her nineties.

Life is like the river: sometimes it sweeps you gently along and sometimes the rapids come out of nowhere.
—Emma Smith

Virginie (rhymes with *HERE's your knee*) Walsh has known both the quiet meanderings and the violent rapids of the river of life.

At ninety-four, Virginie lives in a senior home, but is quite active and very happy. She has earned the right to call *young people*—that is to say, those under sixty—endearing terms such as *dear* and *hon* when addressing them. And for Virginie, addressing others with affection seems as natural as breathing.

Virginie is sharp, engaged in life, engaging to be with, fun, funny, and busy. She is everything one aspires to be as a person nearing life's century mark.

It is tempting to look at Virginie as she is now and presume that she simply floated through life. She seems so unflappable, so content. Such happiness could only have come from a life free of challenges and struggles.

And yet just as a jagged stone is smoothed round when tumbled by the relentless current of the river, so too have Virginie's rough edges been filed away by the river of life.

Life had been flowing along smoothly for both Virginie and her husband, Tom. Then there was an unexpected bend in the river.

Tom worked as an overland truck driver and was often gone for days, if not weeks, at a time. He and Virginie treasured their time at their cabin along the Russian River. Tom drove up to the cabin one night. Virginie was to join him the following morning.

Tom stopped along the way to have a drink at a roadside bar that was a hangout for truckers. After lifting a few beers with friends, he walked back out into the dimly lit parking lot.

"Give me your money or I'll beat the s*** out of you!" the young man demanded. The robber's eyes were filled with rage, and Tom could tell that his threat was sincere. However, Tom was feeling the invincibility of a couple of beers. *I could take him*, he thought. What Tom didn't know was that the thief who stood before him was there to distract him from the real assailant creeping up behind him.

Tom heard a loud, sickening *klunk*. Before he could even connect the sound with the sharp pain in the back of his head, Tom's eyes involuntarily spun upward toward the night sky. His knees buckled, and he fell in a heap onto the cracked asphalt.

Tom couldn't move. With the second blow from the aluminum baseball bat, he lost consciousness.

Virginie was called, and she rushed Tom to a hospital, where he was given a cursory exam followed by a clean bill of health.

However, over the next few days, Tom changed.

"He just wasn't himself," Virginie says. "It's like he moved out and somebody else moved in. I kept telling the doctors, and they said he was fine and that it was just the aftershock of the trauma."

Filled with worry and frustration, Virginie called an old friend who was a doctor in another state. Her friend listened as Virginie described what had happened and how Tom was progressing.

Her friend interrupted brusquely. "Get him to a hospital," he ordered.

"But . . ." Virginie muttered.

He broke in: "I don't care what lie you have to tell him, *get him to a hospital—now!*"

When the doctors reluctantly checked Tom over once again, they discovered two subdural hematomas. Tom's brain was bleeding badly.

Tom spent three long months in the hospital, healing from his attack.

And then the river took another turn.

"Tom couldn't work," Virginie says. "He was hurt too bad, so at age fifty-nine he quit working. I knew I'd better keep him busy or else he might lose his joy of life."

Tom received compensation from a victim's fund and at Virginie's prompting, they used the money to travel. Tom loved the ocean, but Virginie is prone to seasickness. So from the Mississippi to the Nile, Virginie and Tom visited as many of the world's great rivers as they could.

They were very happy together until life's river took yet another turn and Tom died.

Virginie worked through her grief, and then she met Richard. He, too, loved the Russian River and that is where they met. He became Virginie's friend—platonic friend, Virginie is quick to clarify—and the two of them traveled together until the crooked river of life wound another turn, and Richard died as well.

A river travels its course until detoured by an immovable object. When this happens, the river and all of its full force and energy shift without bitterness or complaint toward the new direction. The same is true for Virginie.

After Richard, the unyielding current carried Virginie through the decades. Then, last year, her son Jim died at the age of seventy-one. "I don't care how old you are," she says, "losing a child is hard. But you can't just sit in a chair and wallow in pain—life moves on."

For Virginie, being happy has been a lifelong process of releasing her attachment to life's immovable objects. "You have to accept what is," Virginie says. "Feeling angry and resentful isn't going to make you happy . . . and I want to be happy!"

Virginie offers these three suggestions for enjoying a happier life.

1. **Refuse to be unhappy:** "I see so many unhappy people, and I just don't get it," Virginie says with a weary smile. "It's like some people just *want* to be unhappy. Life is filled with phases, and it's how you adapt that makes you either happy or unhappy."

2. **Force yourself to find something positive:** Most of the things that happen in your life bring positive benefits or, at the very least, have the seeds of positive growth within them.

Seek out what's good in everything. Don't allow your mind to drift into negative territory.

Virginie advises, "If you don't look at life in a positive manner—who are you hurting? No one except yourself! You're just making yourself sad." Clapping her hands together, she adds, "Just do it! Meet circumstances head-on and choose to have a positive attitude and be happy."

3. **Accept where you are in life—it's OK:** Virginie was recently denied the renewal of her driver's license for the first time; so, she sold her car. "What are you going to do?" she says with a big shrug of her shoulders. "You can't change it, you just adapt—you accept it."

Virginie teaches us by example that aging gracefully is celebrating what's left of youth and exploring what's yet to be explored.

HAPPINESS BY THE BOOK

A young man works his way back from the depths of despair to lead the way for others.

How many a man has dated a new era in his life from the reading of a book.
—Henry David Thoreau

Tom slowly opened one eye and gazed about the room. He was looking for *something* familiar to let him know where he was.

The room was small and dirty. Sheets that had once been white but which were now stained a dingy yellow were nailed up unevenly as curtains. The coffee table next to him was piled high with empty beer cans.

Tom attempted to count the cans but found that it made his head hurt even worse. The room reeked of a fetid mixture of fast food, alcohol, cigarette smoke, and rank foot odor.

Tom emitted a long groan as he pulled the small couch pillow over his head to block out the sunlight that filtered in through the grungy sheets. His mouth felt dry and tasted sour. He sat up slowly, feeling a wave of nausea creep over him. His head pounded. Tom reached for a bourbon bottle that sat open and three-quarters empty on the corner of the table.

Tom drank from the bottle greedily until it was empty.

When at last Tom found his shoes, he walked out into the harsh rays of mid-afternoon daylight. He began to meander aimlessly up one street and down another, looking for a place to get some coffee.

Tom Pace was twenty-six. He was tall and handsome and seemed to have everything going for him. He possessed a gift of gab that drew people to him and made him seem very intelligent. In reality, Tom *was* very intelligent, even though he could only read at a fourth-grade level.

Tom had charmed his way through high school and had graduated even though he was functionally illiterate. During the eight years since, Tom had flunked out of two colleges and had held nearly thirty jobs. Now, here he was homeless and unemployed, drinking himself into oblivion each night.

A word began to swirl around in his mind. Tom hated this particular word because he had heard it used to describe him many times: *loser.* Tom spoke the word aloud as he crossed the street to enter a small diner. The word tasted bitter in his mouth, but it seemed, more and more, to be an accurate description of who he was.

Other than the fact that the sun was up, Tom had no idea what time it was. Pressing open the restaurant door, Tom was surprised to find the place nearly empty.

With so many choices, Tom stood a moment and pondered where he might sit. From the back corner of the room, he heard a male voice call his name. Tom walked in the direction of the voice and saw a man seated in a booth with an open book in his hands. He smiled at Tom over the top of the book.

Tom searched through the alcoholic haze of his mind, trying to remember this person but to no avail. They seemed to be about the same age, but, unlike Tom, this man's eyes were clear and he seemed content.

"Hi, Tom," the man said with a genuine smile. Then, waving toward the seat across from him, he invited, "Join me."

Is this guy one of my drinking buddies? Tom wondered as he settled into his seat.

"It's . . . uh, it's been a long time," Tom said, feigning recognition.

Finally, it clicked. This was Scott, an old drinking buddy with whom Tom had spent many nights. But, somehow, he didn't look like Scott.

"You've changed," said Tom.

"You haven't," Scott laughed. "Lemme guess. You just woke up, right, man?"

Tom didn't respond, and Scott laughed again. "Wow, seeing you makes me realize how bad things still are out there," he said.

Once the third cup of coffee kicked in, Tom began to lament how difficult and unfair life was. Scott listened impassively; a serene smile nestled on his face.

After listening to Tom vent for nearly ten minutes, Scott closed the book he had been reading and slid it over to Tom.

Tom glanced down, saw the book, did his best to read the title, and then slid it back to Scott.

Scott immediately slid it once again in Tom's direction.

Tom slid it back.

"Listen, man. You've got to do something different if you want your life to be different," Scott warned. "You've got to take action. Here, take this book and read it. It changed my life."

Tom rose and shoved the paperback into his pocket. He mumbled words of appreciation and shook Scott's hand before leaving the restaurant.

With nowhere to go and nothing to do, Tom found himself sitting on a bus-stop bench. He reached into his pocket and withdrew the book. Now, away from the judgmental eyes of others, he had a chance to slowly and with great difficulty sound out the title: "*The . . . Gr . . . Greatest . . . Mmm . . . Miracle . . . in the World* by Og Man . . . dino."

After deciphering the cover, Tom repeated the title scornfully: "*The Greatest Miracle in the World.*"

With nothing better to do, Tom began to read the book slowly—agonizingly slowly.

Several weeks later, he finally finished. Then he read it again—and again, and again, and again. The book led him to consider that maybe he wasn't a loser after all, but that perhaps the choices he had made put him on this path.

Tom started to hang out with people who were not drinking themselves unconscious. He sought out new friends who took responsibility for their own lives and was surprised to find that they welcomed him into their ranks.

And Tom read. He devoured every book he could find that offered a key to becoming a winner. That was two decades ago, and since then Tom has read more than six hundred such books.

Today, as founder and CEO of PaceButler Corporation—one of the nation's largest resellers of used cell phones—Tom is every inch the winner. He is married, fit, and healthy with two loving daughters. And he hasn't had a drop of alcohol in more than a quarter century. Tom is one of the wealthier people in our society, and he uses his vast financial resources to improve people's lives.

To date, Tom has donated more than a half-million books of various titles to schools, prisons, jails, shelters, mentoring programs, and churches.

"Even though I could barely read at the time," Tom says, "the book Scott gave me was a lifeline. There are millions of people out there who need just such a lifeline, and I'm going to do my best to reach as many of them as I can."

Tom is passionate about his mission. He loves life and is a very happy person. Tom offers a mnemonic device to the many young men he mentors to help them remember his keys to happiness.

"Remember RED," Tom says, offering his secrets for finding happiness.

1. **Read:** Whatever you're going through, someone has been through something similar before and has written a book on how to overcome it. Lean on the knowledge and experience of others.

2. **Exercise:** Tom begins each day with 220 push-ups, and he has run more than forty marathons. "Exercise releases endorphins that make you feel better. And it gives you energy," he says.

3. **Dream:** Your vision of your future is the key determinant of how your life will unfold. "Most people dream small and live small," Tom says. "To live big you've got to dream big."

Tom seeks out "losers" such as his former self as often as he can when hiring for PaceButler. Dozens of men and women owe the redemption of their lives to the example, guidance, and education they have received from Tom.

"And *that* makes me very happy," Tom says with a satisfied smile.

A HAPPY ATTITUDE

A happy attitude gets a man and his family through a serious illness.

Keep your fears to yourself, but share your courage with others.
—Robert Louis Stevenson

David had a secret. However, unless he chose to invite you into his private world and share what was going on, you would have never known this secret. And David wanted it that way.

David Woodcock is in his early thirties and works two jobs. He clears and cleans tables at a restaurant inside his local grocery store, and he cleans theaters and tears tickets at a big multiplex cinema. David is legally blind and takes public transportation wherever he needs to go.

David's secret—known only to a handful of his closest friends and family—was that David had cancer.

Ironically, David himself hadn't known until a few weeks prior. One day, while he and his father were roughhousing, his dad found a lump on his neck. A doctor diagnosed David with

Hodgkin's lymphoma. David had four cancerous tumors growing in his upper body.

"The doctors told me that I would have chemotherapy and that I'd probably be too sick to work," David said. "They told me to plan on taking off until after the treatments."

David smiles and rubs the spot on his neck where the first growth was discovered. "Well, I have rent to pay and other bills, so I just made up my mind to keep working, and I decided it wasn't going to affect me."

David leans forward, and his smile broadens. "And you know what? It didn't."

He was resolved that if he had to go through chemo, then so be it. But he was going to live a normal life throughout the process—a process that would drag on for six months.

David chose to limit the number of people who knew about his cancer because he didn't want to give anyone a chance to bring his attitude down, even if it was out of genuine concern for his well-being. David didn't want people to think of him as "the Cancer Guy." David didn't want to talk about or focus on his illness. He wanted to remain preoccupied with getting well.

David guarded his attitude as his most precious possession throughout the half-year's treatments. "When I was first diagnosed I said to myself, 'I'm going to get through this, and it's not going to get me down.'"

David pats his stomach, "I had no nausea—zero—none. I never missed an hour of work except to go to a doctor's appointment. I didn't get sick because of my attitude."

David's cancer is now in remission, although he insists that it's simply "gone." And who better than David to claim victory over a health challenge? For David, surmounting physical difficulties has been a lifelong endeavor.

David was born with two bad kidneys. He was kept alive until a donor could be found, and as it turned out, his mother was a perfect match. At age one and a half, David became the youngest person ever to receive a kidney transplant up to that time.

Unfortunately, one of the drugs David was given as part of the procedure caused him to develop a severe subdural hematoma. This bleeding in his brain left David with several physical issues and limitations, including partial blindness and weakness on his left side. David experiences sporadic tremors in his left hand, and one of his legs is noticeably shorter than the other.

And yet David, now age thirty-five, seems to stroll under a perpetually sunny sky. He is an extremely happy person. He is one of those people who always has a smile on his face and is forever putting a positive spin on any unfortunate occurrence.

David's happiness is a gift to other people. Whether it's someone sitting alone while having a cup of coffee at the restaurant or a straggling moviegoer exiting a theater, David always goes out of his way to speak to and wish everyone a great day—and he means it.

Some might consider David's jobs menial, but he sees them as great opportunities—not only to earn enough money to pay his bills but also to help others who somehow seem to be missing the point that *life is great*. David sees himself on a mission to raise the happiness level of everyone he meets—even if only a little bit and if it lasts only a short while.

As a result, people are drawn to him and want to be in his company. There are diners who frequent the grocery store restaurant as often as they do simply because they want to bask in David's sunny disposition.

David loves his work, he has a girlfriend he intends to someday marry, he plays basketball, and he has a wide circle of friends. David has taken the cards he was dealt and, with perseverance, has arranged them into a winning hand.

David doesn't believe that he is predisposed to happiness. Rather, he believes that happiness, like fitness, is the result of daily exercise and commitment. David offers three suggestions for happiness.

1. **When you have a problem, tell yourself, "This is just another thing I have to go through:** I might as well do it and get it over with." The stress of trying to ignore a problem is often far more painful than facing and dealing with it head-on. Whatever the challenge—face it, address it, and move past it.

   "When I found out that I had cancer and would have to undergo chemo, I could have gotten angry and cried," David says. "But I didn't. I knew it was going to work out. I said to myself, 'This is just another thing I have to go through. I might as well do it and get it over with.'

   "And when I realized that I didn't have enough money to take off to be sick—that I'd have to work—I could have been upset, but this turned out to be a great blessing. I *had* to make a decision not to be affected by the chemo. And because I decided the chemo wouldn't affect me, it didn't."

2. **Share your vision only with those who can support it:** The list of people who are capable of supporting big dreams is surprisingly quite small. Before you share your hopes and aspirations with someone, ask yourself if this person can support your dream as it stands—without modification—and fully believe that what you desire is possible.

Can this person offer only encouragement and support when you need it—or is this someone who is more often focused on roadblocks and reasons why things won't work out?

"My survival depended on my attitude," David says. "I wasn't going to have anyone who couldn't believe I was going to get well as part of my inner circle in this process."

3. **Attitude is everything:** David says that the best way to elevate and maintain an upbeat attitude is to hang around happy people. "I choose to surround myself with happy people," David says. "I love just spending time with friends. I don't care if it's going to dinner, taking a walk, just sitting and talking. Surrounding myself with other happy people keeps me happy."

HAPPY TO BE OF SERVICE

National Kidney Foundation: www.kidney.org

HAPPY TOGETHER

A woman shares her happiness and love with troubled teen girls.

Hate is not conquered by hate: hate is conquered by love. This is a law eternal.
—the Buddha

Well, *at least everything is spelled correctly,* Marlene muttered to herself.

Marlene Littleton sat down on one of the mismatched dining room chairs in the group home. Marlene knew to seat herself carefully in this particular chair to prevent snagging her pants on the protruding springs. She and her husband, Steve, were houseparents and lived in the home along with their two preschool sons and the approximately eight teenage girls who were placed there.

She had been walking by, carrying yet another load of laundry upstairs, when she noticed that no one was in the dining room. *An empty room in this hectic house is a rare oasis in a vast desert.* She set the laundry basket down and slid out the chair.

The needs of the group house and its young female residents were endless. At the end of each day, Marlene was often both physically and emotionally exhausted. This day had been as difficult as any of the others. She felt as threadbare as the chair cushion beneath her.

Marlene glanced down at the dining room table and a look of shock ran across her face, followed by a dim smile. *Marlene is a bitch!* had been carved deeply into the surface of this most visible piece of furniture.

Marlene traced her index finger along the letters gouged into the table. She thought about the hundreds of girls she had nurtured, comforted, supported, defended, and loved during her five years there. She thought about how mean the girls had been to her the first year, and how nearly every night she had cried herself to sleep alongside Steve in their cramped little sofa bed.

The squeals of teenage girls from the room upstairs snapped Marlene back. She surmised from the excited noise above that the culprit had just informed the other girls of her public act of defiance. She sat back and clasped her hands together as she read the hurtful description of herself once more.

"Ellen!" Marlene shouted raising her face toward the ceiling in an effort to help her voice carry farther.

The room above became instantly still. After the requisite pause children always allow as a subtle testament to their innocence, Ellen shouted back: "What?"

"You and the other girls get down here," Marlene replied. "Right now!"

From above, several voices all mumbled anxiously at the same time.

After nearly a minute, sixteen feet crept tentatively down the steps. The girls stood around, looking awkward and ill at ease.

One girl who had arrived earlier that day just seemed lost—lost and very sad.

Marlene studied the eight girls silently for a moment. Their ages ranged from twelve to sixteen. Every one of them was there against her will. Most of them had experienced things no human being should ever endure—things that could take a lifetime to heal.

Several of the children standing before Marlene had been abused sexually. One girl's mother had dropped her off with neighbors and simply never returned. One only wore long sleeves in an attempt to cover the cigarette burns she'd received from her father. Yet another found her way to Marlene's group home after neighbors reported her being neglected by her crack-addicted mother.

Tears began to well in Marlene's eyes as she exhaled a deep sigh. Her tender heart was near breaking.

It took this rebellious act for Marlene to step back and remember, once again, how fragile and wounded the girls truly were. Whoever did this was lashing out at Marlene because she, herself, was in pain—severe pain.

Marlene cleared her throat, and in her best attempt at sounding stern said, "I wanted you all to know that I've seen the little art project permanently etched into our dining room table."

"Ooooooooo," said a couple of the girls in unison as if rehearsed and on cue. The other girls giggled nervously.

"Anyway," Marlene continued. "As I said, I've seen it and I don't think it's fair."

Marlene paused for effect. These children had been at the hurting end of so many interactions with angry adults that they did not even brace themselves for what was certain to come.

"It's not fair that I be called a bitch for running this house as I do. After all," Marlene continued, a big smile bursting across her face, "Steve makes as many decisions around here as I do."

This wasn't what the girls had expected.

"So," Marlene concluded, "if I'm a bitch, then Steve is a bitch, too."

The smile Marlene beamed into each of their faces exuded compassion. *I will love you no matter what!* Marlene affirmed resolutely in her mind.

"Steve's a bitch," the new girl quietly said. One of the girls giggled and several repeated the comment. Someone suggested carving Steve's name into the table alongside Marlene's. At this, everyone laughed uproariously. Marlene shouted a playful and overly dramatic, "No!" and everyone laughed again.

The girls who walked back up the stairs that evening were not the same girls who had walked down. Whereas every other adult had chosen to treat these children as unlovable when they had given no cause for such treatment, Marlene had shown unconditional love even in the face of criticism and defiance.

Marlene freely admits that she hated her job at the group home in the early years. She was surrounded by so much pain and anger all of the time, and everything she tried was met with rebellion. "Until one day when I decided that I would give these girls the one thing they all needed and none of them had ever had—unconditional love.

"I just opened my heart to the immense pain they had suffered and that continued to haunt them every moment. I realized that I couldn't fix them or heal them, but that I could love them. And suddenly they began to change. They became more helpful and considerate."

When Marlene's attitude shifted, it affected the girls' behavior and the whole culture of the house. Whenever a girl left the house and another moved in, the other girls quickly brought the new one up to speed as to appropriate behavior and the importance of helping out. And it was all because Marlene put into practice the power that will transform anything and anyone—*love*.

Marlene laughs when asked about being a happy person. "Most people are annoyed by how happy I am. I'm so happy people ask what's wrong with me."

Marlene offers the following three tips for happiness.

1. **It's not personal:** Marlene says, "You can choose to reframe something and see it differently if you want to badly enough. Several years ago, I would have gotten angry about the whole table thing. But I learned to see things differently. Those girls were always testing boundaries and acting out, and it had to do with them—with what they had gone through. It had nothing to do with me."

   Give people the benefit of the doubt. Don't take their actions personally.

2. **Everyone has a story:** "The girls taught me this," Marlene admits. "You'd meet these angry, mean, hateful girls who would strike out at others with little or no provocation, and you find yourself wanting to judge them harshly. Then, you spend time with them—you learn their story. You come to realize that those who are hurting someone else are, themselves, hurting."

3. **Look inside for the answers:** "We ask everyone we know what we should do rather than asking and trusting ourselves," Marlene says. "Every girl who came through the

house was unique, and I needed to trust my internal guidance as to how best to work with her."

After eight years, when Marlene's boys became teens themselves, Marlene and Steve moved out of the group home. Marlene went to college and got a degree in counseling and a master's in social work. She still works with children at the group home as well as with others.

When asked what is the most important element in helping someone change, Marlene smiles, "It's the same as it's always been—it's love."

BLESSED TO BE HAPPY

The destructive force of two hurricanes as well as personal setbacks can't dampen the spirits of an amazing survivor.

Blessings star forth forever; but a curse
Is like a cloud—it passes.
—Philip James Bailey

The rain poured in front of Gwen. Meanwhile, the television blared behind her, "If you made the decision to stay, you must stay," the announcer said. "It's too late to evacuate now. We repeat, *stay where you are.*"

Gwen Moliere, known as Miss Gwen to all, stood framed within her open front door; her hands gripped the door's molding as she leaned out into the night.

Her husband, Charles, switched TV channels every few seconds attempting to find—well, he wasn't exactly sure what he hoped to find. All he knew was that it seemed like the end of the world had come, and clicking through the channels provided a distraction, if nothing else.

A percussive explosion off in the distance startled Miss Gwen, and she reflexively covered her head. Just as she was feeling safe enough to lower her hands, another blast—equally loud and terrifying—caused her to shield herself once more.

August 29, 2005: Hurricane Katrina was making landfall and the New Orleans's levee had begun to collapse. The explosions Miss Gwen had heard were twenty-foot-high levee walls being ripped apart.

Miss Gwen, Charles, and their twenty-two-year-old son, Raynell, stood mouths agape as they stared out their front door. They were transfixed with terror. In a flash, their minds processed a thousand things they might do, and none of them would ensure their safety.

Charles did the most logical thing he could in a totally illogical situation. He pulled his wife inside and forced the door closed. They all stood soaked and terrified as the water climbed past their ankles. Not knowing what else to do, Charles bolted the door.

The water quickly penetrated the exterior wall and rushed to fill up the space between it and the drywall. Miss Gwen describes the moment as if she has relived it a thousand times in her mind. "All of a sudden, the water starts pouring in through every crack in the house. It came in through nail holes in the wall where we had moved pictures, cracks in the dry wall, spaces around the windows—everywhere!"

The pressure inside the walls was building as the water rose rapidly. Soon, water was spewing from higher cracks and new, larger cracks began to form. Any second now the water could either break through the interior walls, crushing them to death, or the raging torrent would rip the house from its foundation and wipe it and its inhabitants from the face of the earth.

Recovering from the paralysis of panic, Raynell grabbed two unlikely objects—a blanket and a hammer—and pushed his mother and father toward the door to their attic. Miss Gwen stopped here and there along the way as she swept framed pictures and photo albums up into her arms; the water was at her thighs.

The trio rapidly ascended the stairs to the attic, not knowing if the water would rise above their roofline and drown them like rats trapped inside a sinking ship.

As it turned out, Raynell's selection of what to take into the attic was brilliant. The blanket was used to keep itchy attic insulation away from their skin. The hammer could be used to create an emergency exit should they need one.

Within hours, the outside temperature soared above one hundred degrees and the humidity settled in at a sticky 70 percent.

Inside, the attic was like a wet oven. Miss Gwen nearly fainted from heat exhaustion. Raynell used the hammer to tear a hole in the roof for ventilation. That hole soon became an escape hatch as the three of them climbed out onto the roof, and there—like many of New Orleans's poorest families whose lives were shattered by this monstrous storm—they lived for five agonizing days.

All around them foul, black water rushed by day and night, carrying in its maw the entire range of human possessions as well as the bloated bodies of the dead. Here and there, alligators feasted on the remains of both humans and animals.

Throughout the ordeal, Miss Gwen reminded herself constantly that she was blessed. Blessed to be alive. Blessed to be able to help rescue an eighty-year-old woman who would have died stuck in her own attic. Blessed to have food and water. Even as she broiled in the unrelenting sun, Miss Gwen told herself that she was blessed.

And nearly a week after they mounted their roof, Miss Gwen knew she was blessed when a helicopter lifted them all to safety.

After Katrina, Miss Gwen and her family relocated to Galveston, Texas, where she and Charles got jobs and obtained a new house while they waited for their city and their home to be rebuilt. Miss Gwen felt blessed by this as well.

Then, on September 12, 2008, Hurricane Ike struck Galveston. For a second time a hurricane washed away their home and most of their belongings. And still, Miss Gwen considered herself blessed.

An infection in Miss Gwen's leg did not respond to treatment; doctors had to amputate it to save her life. And, as always, Miss Gwen reminded herself that she was blessed.

She and Charles separated and divorced, yet even during this Miss Gwen considered herself blessed.

Returning home to New Orleans, Miss Gwen discovered that the contractor she had hired to rebuild her home had run off with her money. So Miss Gwen took stock of her life, weighed the good and the bad, and came to the conclusion that she was blessed.

A few months later, another contractor accepted Miss Gwen's money and never began work. Next, thieves who had swarmed New Orleans like locusts after the hurricane stole the materials purchased to rebuild her home. Such unfortunate incidents happened over and over, and yet every time difficulty and tragedy came to call at Miss Gwen's door, it found her smiling and giving thanks and counting her blessings.

Miss Gwen's happiness is absolute and unshakable. Here are her three tips for happiness.

1. **Count your blessings:** It took eight years for Miss Gwen to finally return to her home in New Orleans. She moved in during the oppressive heat of summer only to discover that her central air-conditioning unit had been stolen. Fearing other thieves and vandals, she didn't dare leave her home while a replacement unit was acquired and installed.

   So for three weeks Miss Gwen boiled in the heat. All the while, she gave thanks for her life, her friends, her health, her family—anything and everything that enhanced her life.

   For Miss Gwen, the glass isn't half-full; it is perpetually overflowing.

2. **Know that you are stronger than you imagine:** "After everything that happened to me," Miss Gwen says with a broad grin, "I think I should be crazy. I should be flat-out *cuckoo*. But I got through it. When you go through something tough, it shows you just how strong you are."

3. **Get something out of everything:** "It's not your loss that's important," Miss Gwen advises, "It's *what you do* in the midst of your loss.

   "Did you learn something? Well, then, don't think about what you lost; think about what you gained. Even if the only thing you gained is wisdom, you gained!"

   Miss Gwen concludes by explaining the reason for her own happiness. "Whenever I meet anyone, I always remind them to 'Have a blessed day.' And you know why I say that? 'Cause you and me—we're the lucky ones. We got chosen to wake up this morning. Do you realize how many people didn't get that call? Do you know how many people went to bed last night and didn't get chosen to live today? You were blessed before you even got out of bed because you woke up—never forget that."

HAPPY CARVED IN STONE

An artist shares pieces of his beloved homeland with the planet.

Ten measures of beauty descended to the world, nine were taken by Jerusalem.
—The Talmud, *Kiddushin* 49b

S am Nachum lay in bed recovering from major surgery on his neck.

It was 1994, Sam was thirty-seven, and he'd finally found a doctor capable of performing the delicate and dangerous operation. The physician had warned him that he would be bedridden for a full year following the procedure.

Lying in bed for a year—that would be difficult for anyone, but it was especially challenging for Sam.

Sam had always been a *doer*. He worked with his hands. He created beautiful stained-glass works of art. As grateful as he was for having the surgery that delivered him from constant pain,

Sam felt like the year on his back was ticking by at a glacier's pace.

Sam clicked through the TV channels as his three children, Benjamin, Rachel, and Elan—ages ten, eight, and six, respectively—played at the foot of his bed. Sam's body was to have only limited movement for twelve months. During that time it seemed as if his mind became all the more active to compensate for his immobility.

Sam pressed the "Up Channel" button on the remote. Images flashed rapidly on the screen as he briefly previewed each station. Something on CNN caught his interest, so he stopped channel surfing. There, once again, the news in America and around the world was about Sam's home country of Israel.

In this already very violent part of the world, 1994 was proving to be an excessively violent year. Nearly two hundred Israelis and Palestinians had been killed. Some of the deaths were the result of military operations; others were brutal and vicious attacks led by individuals.

Only a year earlier, hopes had been high for real and lasting peace in the Middle East when Israeli Prime Minister Yitzhak Rabin, Israeli Foreign Minister Shimon Peres, and Palestinian leader Yasser Arafat came together to produce the Oslo Accords, which laid out a plan for peaceful coexistence.

In 1994, the three men were jointly awarded the Nobel Peace Prize. And yet the violence continued.

On the TV screen, Sam could see mobs of angry Palestinians throwing stones at civilians and Israeli soldiers. His heart ached for his countrymen.

Sam drew in a deep breath and pressed the "Off" button. He tossed the remote onto a pile of magazines that lay next to his hip, and then stared up at the ceiling. Sam sighed a long, disquieted sigh.

He closed his eyes, and his mind drifted back to his boyhood home of Malha, Israel. Sam was one of five children raised in a twenty-by-twenty-foot stone hut. His home was in the poorest and most violent section of Malha, which in 1967 was part of the violently disputed West Bank.

Although Sam had been raised in a cramped home with a dirt floor, surrounded by violence and death, he felt pride in his family's home. It had been constructed of stone from the heartland of his family, his culture, his faith.

"This isn't right," Sam said.

"I'm sorry . . . what?" asked Sam's wife, Dana, as she carried a basket full of freshly folded laundry into the room.

"*It isn't right*," Sam repeated. "It doesn't matter what country you are in, if you see news about Jerusalem, you're going to see violence. And now people watching the news are seeing Jerusalem's natural beauty—her stone—being used as a weapon."

Rocking a little from side to side to get more comfortable, Sam said for a third time, "It just isn't right."

Dana set the laundry basket gently down next to her husband. "So, what are you thinking?" she asked.

"I think that for most people, especially here in the United States, Israel seems like some distant war-torn third world kind of place. People hear about Israel all the time, but only in the context of people killing or hurting one another. Israel has become synonymous with violence."

After a pause, Sam continued: "And the stone—the stone there is so beautiful."

"I agree," said Dana.

"I'm going to import the stone and sell it here in the United States," Sam declared.

And that declaration began what would become known as JerUSAlem Stone. Sam had no idea where or how to begin, but he and Dana got started immediately. Sam did what he could from his bed, and when he felt able, he got up and set to work. The couple mortgaged their house, flew to Israel, and began calling on quarries. Sam, who still had a long road ahead to recovery, wore a neck brace to all of the meetings. In short order, they had struck deals and began promoting the use of Jerusalem stone in countertops, walkways, bathrooms, fireplaces, and more in the United States.

Several years ago, many New Thought churches, such as Unity, Centers for Spiritual Living, and others began an annual ritual known as the White Stone Ceremony, which is typically held in early January.

In a White Stone Ceremony, each person is asked to prayerfully discern one specific word (e.g., *love*, *forgiveness*, *humility*, *happiness*, *faith*) that will serve as their guiding principle for the coming year. The word is then written on a piece of white stone and placed in a prominent place to serve as a reminder.

Sam's stone from Jerusalem is the universal favorite for this ceremony, and each year he prepares and sends out more than twenty-five thousand tiles about the size of a man's thumb. Sam is honored, happy, and proud that his stone is being used for such a sacred and transformative purpose.

Sam's work is his passion. He gets to share his creativity as well as part of his beloved Israel with people around the world now that his business is approximately 80 percent international. And people love being in Sam's cheerful presence.

Sam offers three tips for being happy.

1. **Put things into perspective:** Sam says, "Whenever I hear someone complaining about how *bad* their day is, I say, 'What if you were dead now? Wouldn't you trade being dead for this so-called bad day? Of course you would, so stop complaining—you're alive, so find a way to feel joy.'"

2. **Allow other people to love you:** "Many Jewish people say, 'I hate the Germans' or 'I hate the Arabs.' They are angry because of how they or their ancestors were treated. Well, there are Germans and Arabs who do *not* hate us—and they want the pain of the past gone as badly as we do. These people have the capacity and the desire to love us. When we stew in our hatred and anger over what people have done in the past, we sever our connection to other people who, although they might be from the same country or are of the same religion as people who have been cruel and oppressive, are not that way. We have to open ourselves to new relationships with them, based on love."

3. **Don't just exist; live life—every day!** "We are just visitors on this planet—every moment is precious," Sam says. "If that's the case, ask yourself what percent of your life you want to spend angry at others? When you total up your moments of life, how much of it would you want to have spent arguing, depressed, or resentful?

   "Me? I want to look back and see mostly happy, productive moments."

Sam makes the statement most common to happy people: "Happiness is an inside job."

To cultivate your own happiness, remember the words of venerated Rabbi Yeruchom Levovitz: "A truly happy person does not allow his happiness to be dependent on any external factor over which he may not have control."

THE LANGUAGE OF HAPPINESS
In Hebrew, the word for happy is *simcha* (SIM-kha).

HAPPINESS IS A WARM PUPPY

A mother commits theft to help her son regain a normal life.

The moment one definitely commits oneself, then Providence moves too.
—William Hutchison Murray

L ucy squatted down, crept silently forward, and then stood just high enough to peer through the glass panes in the large double doors that separated her from the object she desired.

When she saw no one was there, Lucy stood a little taller. Ahead she could see an empty hallway. She knew there were people around—lots of them, but Lucy had timed her theft precisely to limit the likelihood of running into any of them. After weeks of practically living in this building, Lucy knew its rhythms; she knew its routines. And she knew precisely when to act.

Now was the time.

Lucy placed her palms on the right-hand door and slowly, very slowly pressed forward with the weight of her body. The twin rubber gaskets that lined the two doors' inner edges slid soundlessly apart, and Lucy stepped into the hall.

It's not bad enough that I'm stealing, Lucy thought to herself. *I'm stealing a walker from the geriatric unit of a hospital.*

Lucy could hear several voices speaking in hushed tones as the staff shared status reports for each patient. Lucy prayed that there had been no stragglers to the meeting.

Sometimes, she knew, a nurse or aid would get busy with a patient and arrive late for these meetings. If that happened, Lucy might be spotted, and she would seem suspicious, especially at this late hour.

Lucy stopped outside the door to the first room and listened intently. Hearing nothing, she leaned in and saw that the room was unoccupied. Lucy tiptoed to the next room. Listening once more, she could hear the rhythmic sound of someone gently snoring.

Lucy did her best to slink silently as a cat into the room. As her eyes adjusted to the dim light, she glanced about hoping to see a walker that she could steal.

As Lucy turned to leave that room, her hip bumped into something.

Feeling the object with both hands, Lucy whispered, "Pay dirt." She quickly folded the walker and carried it out of the room. She strode confidently back up the hallway, through the double doors, and took the elevator back down to the third floor, where her son Jesse had been living for many weeks.

Jesse says, "The next morning my mom put her arms around my waist and pulled me up. She said, 'Let's do it!' And I took about two steps with the walker. It wasn't much, but I walked!"

Jesse was nineteen and had Guillain–Barré syndrome (GBS). GBS begins in a person's extremities and migrates throughout the body. Patients say that GBS tingles like your hands and feet have fallen asleep. In time, paralysis sets in. GBS is the number one cause of non-trauma-related paralysis.

When the doctor gave Jesse his diagnosis, his entire family had cried—but not Jesse. "I was young," he says, grinning. "I didn't believe anything *anyone* told me, so I didn't believe the doctors, either. I just knew I'd walk again."

Jesse's mother fed off his confident energy and was soon completely enrolled in Jesse's commitment to beat GBS.

Medical authorities told Jesse that he would end up wheelchair bound and would be too weak to push the chair himself. Jesse asked if exercising his upper body might not maintain his strength so that he could push his wheelchair, but he was told that trying to build his body while it was slowly being atrophied by GBS was a waste of time.

Jesse ignored the doctors, and Lucy began to sneak light dumbbells into his room. When no one was looking, Jesse would train with the weights, or he and Lucy would toss a three-pound bag back and forth. Within weeks, Jesse was pushing his wheelchair up and down the hall.

When the doctors saw how well he was progressing, Jesse confessed to his secret training. The doctors encouraged Jesse to continue with his exercises.

Lucy, having fully bought into Jesse's vision of recovery, requested the use of a walker as the next step toward Jesse recovering fully. Her request was denied.

No, the doctors had spoken; Jesse would be in a wheelchair. The upper body exercises might allow him to push the chair, but

Jesse was paralyzed from the thighs down and that's how he and the family should expect him to be.

That's when Jesse and Lucy decided that if they were not to be given a walker, they would get one by whatever means necessary—even if it meant stealing one from the Geriatric Unit in the middle of the night.

"My mom would hide the walker in the closet until we were pretty sure no one was around," Jesse says with a smile. "Then she'd haul it out, stand me up, and we'd walk. Once I got good, we showed the doctor."

The doctor was amazed. Against the odds, Jesse had exercised and trained his body, and with the aid of the walker was able to move around the hospital.

Before the doctor could finish praising Jesse for his progress with the walker, Lucy squared herself in front of the physician and said coolly, "Now, we want a cane."

This time, Lucy didn't have to commit petty theft to get what she wanted. And Jesse transitioned in short order from the walker to a cane. And then he set the cane aside.

Twelve years have passed since Jesse was first diagnosed. GBS has a 50 percent relapse rate, but thus far Jesse is fine. He lives with his puppy in Queens, New York, and works with the Department of Social Services to help create safe living environments for children. Jesse loves his job.

"I'd be lying if I said I was really happy when they told me at nineteen that I'd never walk," Jessie says. "But overall, before then and especially now, I'm very happy. I can walk today because I chose to walk. I'm happy because I choose to be happy."

Jesse offers these three happiness tips.

1. **Reflection is important:** "Reflect on your life but not just the good times," Jesse advises. "Think about the bad times, too,

and how you overcame them. It makes you realize you can get through anything."

2. **Expand on your current happiness:** "What makes you smile?" Jesse asks. "Notice what causes you to smile and feel happy. Then make a commitment to do whatever that is as often as possible."

3. **Buy a puppy:** "I never wanted a puppy," Jesse confesses. "It was given to me. But there are times that no one can comfort me but him. I will come home feeling a little low, and he knows. When he jumps in my lap, it's pure, safe, unconditional love.

   "Then I feel better and things don't bother me. I find myself happy again, and that's where I want to be."

   Jesse smiles and says again, "Yep, I want to be happy."

HAPPY TO BE OF SERVICE

Guillain–Barré syndrome support: www.gbs-cidp.org

THE TRUTH WILL SET YOU FREE

A woman confronts her mother in an attempt to heal the wounds of her past.

Tell truth and shame the devil.
If thou have power to raise him, bring him hither,
And I'll be sworn I have power to shame him hence.
—William Shakespeare, *Henry IV, Part 1*

M arilyn's car crested the summit of one of the tallest and most majestic of Kentucky's Cumberland Mountains.

The scenery passing on all sides was stunning, but Marilyn barely noticed. For more than an hour, her mind had withdrawn into itself.

Marilyn Gibson's mother, Ruby, sat alongside her in the passenger seat of the silver Chevrolet Cavalier. Ruby prattled on, oblivious to the fact that Marilyn had long ago mentally checked out of their conversation.

Marilyn was actively engaged in a conversation in her own mind, one she'd had hundreds—no, thousands—of times. There, in the safe confines of her own head, Marilyn would confront her mother. She faced her powerfully but without anger or resentment. In the conversation that ran solely in her mind, Marilyn would press her mother until she confessed—confessed that she believed what had happened to Marilyn.

A voice, which Marilyn can only describe as sacred, whispered in her ear. *Now's the time.* Without giving herself an opportunity to chicken out, Marilyn switched on her right-turn signal and pulled the car over at a scenic lookout.

"Why are we stopping *here*?" Ruby inquired. Ruby's real curiosity was not about why Marilyn had pulled the car over, but why her monologue had been interrupted.

The car was already beginning to feel cramped and void of oxygen. Marilyn opened the windows to allow fresh air in. She drank in the mountain air as if it were nectar. Feeling as if she were about to dive headlong off one of the peaks that filled the horizon before them, Marilyn turned her entire upper body to face her mother.

Ruby looked bewildered. She smiled nervously.

An ethereal calm surrounded Marilyn like a warm fog. She felt as if she were on the verge of freedom. One way or the other, she'd be free.

"Mom," Marilyn said with a genuine smile. "This car isn't moving until you say you believe me."

"Oh my God!" said Ruby. "Oh, my God! This again?"

Neither Marilyn's gaze nor her smile wavered.

"You need to let this go, Marilyn," her mother warned. "You're ... what ... thirty-five years old, now? Give it a rest already!"

"Mom . . ."

Ruby spat protest after protest; her tone of voice bouncing from rage to panic and back again. "Start the car. *Start this car!* Let me out. *You're holding me against my will!*"

"I'm not holding you anywhere, and you can get out and walk if you want," Marilyn said, her voice smooth as glass. "I'm simply informing you that this car stays where it's parked until you say you believe me."

"Well I *don't* believe you," Ruby whined. "Your grandfather was a good man. He helped me take care of you and your sisters while your father was in Korea."

"Mom," Marilyn said soothingly.

"I was a stay-at-home mother with three daughters!" Ruby wailed.

"I'm not saying I blame you," Marilyn continued. "I'm not. I'm saying that it's important that you believe me."

"Believe you about what?" Ruby screamed, her shrill voice amplified by the car's small interior.

"Believe me when I tell you that your father—my grandfather—sexually abused me. He molested me, repeatedly—sometimes daily—when I was just a little girl."

Ruby rattled the door handle, her hands shaking feverishly. "Let me out!" she demanded.

"Just tell me you believe me, Mom," Marilyn said.

Ruby began to cry. Her plaintive tears shifted into heaving sobs. Ruby gasped for breath as her shoulders heaved.

Marilyn withheld her natural tendency to comfort her mother. She knew that if she hugged her mother or even squeezed her hand, this moment could be lost and one like it might never come again.

Marilyn spoke kindly to her mother, who was now near hysteria. "Say you believe me . . . say you believe me."

Ruby beat the dashboard with her hand as she wept. Marilyn was a master sculptor's homage to serenity. "Come on, Mom," Marilyn encouraged.

Finally, her voice low and faint, Ruby admitted, "He touched you . . . okay? He touched you. I believe you."

"He did a *lot* more than just touch me!" Marilyn interjected.

"He *touched* you!" Ruby repeated. This was the strongest indictment she was capable of mustering against her father, Marilyn's grandfather.

"He touched you," she said again. This time, more softly. Then, she admitted, "And he touched me, too."

Marilyn looked in the rearview mirror. There she still saw the face of that innocent little girl being beckoned to sit on her grandfather's lap. There, in the mirror, Marilyn gazed deeply into her own eyes and smiled broadly.

Sensing that the time was at last right, Marilyn reached over and squeezed her mother's hand. Mother and daughter exchanged a brief, awkward hug. Marilyn started the car and merged back into traffic.

Marilyn felt as if her wounds—which had seemed like indelible marks scratched into her soul—were beginning to fade, if only a little. While she drove, Marilyn peered over at her mother who sat wiping her eyes. Rather than being angry with her, Marilyn felt compassion for that abused little girl that was now her tortured mother.

It's been twenty-six years since Marilyn had the courage to confront her mother and begin her own healing in earnest. People who know both Marilyn and her story have great difficulty in reconciling the two.

Marilyn bears a perpetual smile that begins in her heart and pours out through her eyes. Marilyn shines love with her entire being and others respond. She has become a spiritual mentor for several women and regularly counsels and encourages them. She models that healing from deep wounds is possible and assures clients that happiness awaits those willing to work through the aftereffects of trauma.

Marilyn says that almost everyone is wounded in some way— some more so than others. But regardless of the traumatic experience a person has gone through, there are things to remember that can bring you back around to happiness. She offers these three things to keep in mind.

1. **It's never your fault:** "Abusers abuse," Marilyn says with a shrug of her shoulder. "It's not personal to the abused person, and there is freedom in realizing that."

   Marilyn goes on to say that there is power in not taking responsibility for *anyone's* negative actions toward you. In most cases, people are reacting out of their own fear and pain. So if a person is rude to you at the grocery store or if someone cuts you off in traffic, it's not your issue—it's theirs. To be happy, let it go.

2. **Know that the Great Spirit has your back:** From the time Marilyn was a little girl, she has felt a loving presence—a sacred energy that has protected her. "Even in my darkest times," she says, "I never felt alone. Something . . . be it God, or whatever, was there, and I was aware of it. It kept me alive then, and it keeps me happy and fulfilled today."

   Marilyn cultivates her connection with what she calls the Great Spirit through prayer and meditation.

3. **Recovery is a process:** It has taken decades for Marilyn to move through her anger, resentment, and grief to find freedom and happiness. "It takes commitment and patience," Marilyn advises. "But healing your past brings great gifts,

like compassion. I'm far more compassionate today, and it's because I've had to be gentle and compassionate with myself."

HAPPY TO BE OF SERVICE
If you suspect child abuse, call 1-800-4-A-Child (800-422-4453).

ETERNAL HAPPINESS

An elementary school principal maintains happiness through his connection with his family.

All farewells should be sudden, when forever,
Else they make an eternity of moments,
And clog the last sad sands of life with tears.
—Lord Byron

Patrick Farnan woke up, rolled over, and gazed into the green glow of the hotel's bedside clock. It was 1:07 a.m. *That's odd,* he thought to himself.

Patrick is an elementary school principal, and he was at a conference for educators. Patrick rarely, if ever, awoke during the middle of the night—even if he were in an unfamiliar bed as he was that evening.

Shifting his gaze to the ceiling, Patrick tried to understand why his mind had disturbed his slumber. Doing a quick mental inventory, he found that he was fully prepared to introduce the conference speaker the following morning and, so far as he knew, there were no niggling tasks requiring his attention.

Sliding his feet to the floor, Patrick switched on the bedside lamp, and stood slowly. He walked over to the window and gazed into the night sky radiantly adorned with stars.

Patrick felt comforted knowing that his son, Colby, was under the same sky even if he was seven thousand miles away. Patrick yawned loudly and returned to his bed.

At that moment, twenty-two-year-old Private First Class Colby Farnan stepped out into the heat of Bagdad's city streets. Colby was deployed to Camp Taji, and this was his fifth day in Iraq.

Colby and two other army privates were leaving on what is known as a "right seat ride" with another soldier who would soon be returning stateside. A right seat ride is when a soldier experienced with a location and the duties to be performed shares this knowledge with the new guys.

The four men walked down the street toward a narrow artificial irrigation ditch. Here and there buildings were either destroyed or scorched from street-side bomb blasts.

Colby's every sense was hypervigilant. His eyes repeatedly scanned from left to right, and then from up to down. He was keenly aware of every movement and sound. As he looked at his buddies, he could tell that they, too, were on high alert.

"You feel that?" the seasoned soldier asked. "That feeling you've got right now—you feel it? Don't *ever* lose that feeling, man. If you're not scared, you're not being cautious enough."

The veteran soldier pointed in the direction of a building that appeared to have once been a hotel and which now had all of its windows blown out; an inverted pyramid of soot stretched halfway up its exterior.

"Guys who get lax, get dead," he warned.

The blast that destroyed the old hotel—just like the ones that scorched and destroyed the other buildings—were caused by an improvised explosive device (IED). An IED is typically pieced together from old bomb casings or other scrap. It is called an improvised device because it is not automatic; it has to be detonated by someone using a remote control of some kind.

As Colby and his friends walked, he noticed a man intently watching them from about sixty meters south of their position. The man looked like any other Iraqi mulling about the busy street, but something about him seemed unsettling.

"What do you make of that?" Colby asked the seasoned soldier.

"What?" the soldier asked, turning to look in the direction Colby was pointing.

"That guy back there, he's . . ." Colby's voice trailed off. He began to raise his weapon as the man reached into a pocket of his *thawb*—the traditional garment of Arabic men.

Time stopped.

This Iraqi man had been busy. He had arisen that morning before dawn and planted an IED in the crest of a palm tree that had been cut down to about four feet in height. The man had stood all morning watching American soldiers come close—but in his estimation, not close enough.

Finally, his patience had paid off when Colby and his compatriots walked right up to the device.

The man's grubby thumb found the garage door opener he had concealed inside his pocket, and he pushed the button. Concussive shock waves erupted out in all directions at 1,600 feet per second, leveling everything and killing everyone within forty meters.

Back at the hotel in the United States, Colby's father, Patrick, awoke for a second time. As he showered and dressed, Patrick switched on the cable news station. Pope John Paul II had died, and the network was celebrating the pontiff's accomplishments and speculating as to his legacy.

Then, as if they were a footnote, the announcer added twelve words before going to commercial, "And, in Bagdad today, three US soldiers were killed while on patrol."

Patrick gave no more thought to the story about the fallen soldiers than he had the one about the Pope's death. He switched off the TV and headed for the conference.

"They really do come up and knock on your door," says Patrick. "An officer arrived and told my wife, Deana, that Colby was dead. My sister-in-law then called me."

Patrick and Deana were in shock for months after Colby's death. "She is a nurse, and I am a degreed educator," Patrick says, "but we couldn't figure out what to eat for dinner."

A year previously, Patrick's father, whom he loved dearly, had died of Parkinson's disease. Now, his only son had been struck down by war.

Patrick found comfort throwing himself into supporting Deana and their daughter, Kristen, through their grief.

Two deaths in two years was devastating. Then the following year, the cold and impersonal hand of death touched Finn, Patrick's twenty-two-month-old grandson. He had fallen asleep in his crib and slipped from life, a victim of sudden infant death syndrome (SIDS).

Within the span of twenty-four months, Patrick had lost his father, his son, and his grandson. Such deeply painful events—especially in such rapid succession—have forever altered the lives of some.

But not Patrick.

Patrick has always been and still is a happy guy. Of course he grieved the loss of each of his loved ones, and he misses them to this day. But he has not let their deaths diminish his life. In fact, just the opposite.

Here are Patrick's recommendations for being happy.

1. **Believe that the deceased loved ones are still with you:** Every morning, Patrick puts on a bracelet that reminds him of Finn. Next, he drapes Colby's dog tags around his neck. Throughout the day, he intentionally feels his son's and his grandson's presence and his focus is on them.

   "I'm not angry that they're dead," he says. "I'm focusing on the fact that they live on and are still with me."

2. **If they were close, keep them close:** "I measure my success and failure each day by whether I believe Colby and Finn would be proud of me," Patrick says. "It's actually lessened my stress and made me even *more* happy to shift my focus on whether I have made them proud. And it keeps me feeling close to them."

3. **It happened—now find a way to bring something good out of it:** First, Patrick planted a tree in Colby's honor. Next, he erected a flagpole. Then, Colby's sister, Kristen, told the family about Battlefield Crosses. A Battlefield Cross or Fallen Soldier's Cross is a symbolic replacement for a gravesite cross. They cost $5,000 each.

   Not satisfied by purchasing one just for Colby, Patrick and his family organized the annual Walk to Remember that raised money to purchase thirty-three crosses for fallen soldiers.

"I probably wouldn't have done this if Colby hadn't been killed," Patrick says with a smile. "But out of our loss came some good for a lot of people, and for that, I'm pretty happy."

HAPPY TO BE OF SERVICE

www.USO.org/Families-of-the-Fallen-Support

A CITIZEN OF HAPPINESS

After discovering he's no longer welcome in his home country, a boy and his family survive for decades before immigrating to the United States.

And I urge you to please notice when you are happy, and exclaim or murmur or think at some point, "If this isn't nice, I don't know what is."
—Kurt Vonnegut, *A Man Without a Country*

Ten-year-old Santosh Biswa stared in disbelief, trying to comprehend what his father had said. Letting the shock settle for a moment, Santosh asked his father meekly, "You mean I don't get to go to school tomorrow?"

Santosh's father stared at him. In his father's eyes Santosh could see so many expressions flashing—rage, fear, resignation, hatred. The well of tears that pooled in his father's large brown eyes made Santosh afraid.

Santosh had been born and raised in Bhutan in the midst of an ongoing civil unrest. Bomb blasts were common, and Santosh, still three years away from being a teenager, knew more than a dozen people who had lost their lives to violence.

"Not just tomorrow," Santosh's mother said, caressing her son's cheek with the back of her hand. "You can't return to school—ever."

Santosh didn't understand. He looked from his father to his mother and back again.

With the heat of his anger, Santosh's father crushed a small sheaf of papers in his right hand. He crumpled the pages as if trying to strangle lifeless the words written upon them.

"It seems that we are no longer citizens of Bhutan," his father said through gritted teeth.

"But . . . um . . . but I was born here," Santosh said, adding in a whisper: "We were *all* born here."

A long silence hung in the air. Then, Santosh's father dropped to his knees and began to weep. Santosh's mother rushed to her husband and dropped beside him. She threw her arms around his neck and began to wail. Not knowing what else to do, Santosh joined his parents on the floor. They pulled him and his younger brother and sister close, holding on as if for dear life itself.

It was 1992 and the Bhutanese government had taken a census. They had then used the census to categorize their citizens. Information about each person's ethnicity and the languages they spoke was compiled along with several other complex characteristics deemed classified by the government. The result was that every adult citizen was codified into a numeric ranking ranging from one to seven.

Anyone fortunate to score a one was designated to be among the "purest" citizens of Bhutan. The closer one's ranking came to seven, the more questionable was that person's citizenship.

Based on the government's calculations, Santosh's father was ranked a seven—the lowest possible designation—while his mother was listed as a three. The resulting impact was that the entire family had their Bhutanese citizenship revoked.

The Biswa family and hundreds of thousands of others just like them were designated persona non grata by their government. They were noncitizens, having no right to public services and no right to own property. Parents were banned from working, and children were barred from school.

With no opportunity to work, families everywhere began to starve. Life was bleak.

And then the women began to disappear.

It was all done under the guise of "official procedure." The army or police would show up at a family's home with a warrant to bring the entire family in for questioning. Then the members of the family would be separated. Ultimately, the men would be released and the women would remain.

The women would never be seen or heard from again—their fates unknown. There were rumors as to what happened to wives and daughters seized by officials—vile, grotesque rumors—but no female ever returned to verify or deny them.

The Biswas had no money and could not work. Just a few weeks prior, they had been well off by Bhutanese standards. Both parents had good jobs, while Santosh, his brother, and his sister were all doing well in school. Yes, they lived in the middle of a violence-ridden city, but, over time, one becomes numb to such things.

Now it was as if they had been erased from existence, and their bodies reflected their diminishing status. Things couldn't get worse. Until they did.

Santosh's uncle sent the family a letter stating that he had been forced to sell their ancestral land to the government. An army of men showed up on the land, and an officer presented Santosh's uncle with a document. As several rifles pointed at his uncle's head, he signed the paper with a shaking hand. He was paid less than 1 percent of the land's value and was then driven off.

Not only was this the family's ancestral land, it had been the Biswas's financial ace in the hole. If things got too bad, they could sell the land, and even after dividing the money among extended family members, they could have survived. Now they were truly destitute.

Even the family members' names were changed to reflect their new immigrant status. Santosh—whose name had meant *satisfied*—found his name changed to Gobar, which means *cow dung* in Bhutanese Dzongkha.

No longer legal citizens, the Biswa family, and others like them, were deported from Bhutan. Because Santosh's—that is to say Gobar's—family spoke Nepalese, they, along with more than one hundred thousand of those who had been their fellow citizens, were deported to Nepal.

Nepal found itself on the receiving end of an invasion of people—people they were ill prepared to feed and shelter. A makeshift refugee camp was hastily assembled in the jungles of Nepal. No longer welcome in their homeland, these people found themselves unwanted guests of another country.

Again, they were not allowed to work. If they were caught working, they were tortured. If, however, they were able to get employment under the table, they were paid one-tenth of what a native Nepalese would receive for the same labor.

Gobar and his family endured the disease, famine, and filth of the refugee camp for nearly twenty years. During that time, twenty-one bilateral conventions were held between the Bhutanese and the Nepalese. All of the discussions went full circle to agree on one thing—these people were the other country's problem.

During his more than two decades in the refugee camp, Gobar never lost his optimism and his love of life. When he was at last relocated to the United States along with his family, Gobar was ecstatic.

Gobar now works as a waiter in a Chinese restaurant supporting himself, Buddha—his wife of four years—and their two-year-old son, Anugra. "In the United States, so long as you work hard, you can be successful," he says.

When he came to the United States, Gobar expected to meet a lot of happy people and was surprised to discover that most Americans seem to be unhappy. He feels that becoming happier is possible for everyone, and he offers these three suggestions.

1. **Don't fan the flames of discord:** Gobar says, "It seems that when Americans have trouble, they make a big mess by talking to everyone except the person they have a problem with. Whereas, if we have trouble in our family, we resolve it—directly."

2. **Play with children:** "If you have a problem, go play with your children," Gobar advises. "Children are always happy. They give you a different perspective. When you're with children, sorrow and sadness will go away."

3. **Don't let your problems be bigger than your happiness:** Gobar offers, "We have a saying: If you have trouble today,

resolve it tomorrow so that the day after tomorrow, you don't have any trouble."

As for the name assigned to him from the census, Gobar decided to keep it. Not only does it mean *cow dung,* it also means *sacred mountain.* Gobar sees his early life as *cow dung* fertilizing the fields to raise up a *sacred mountain of happiness.*

THE LANGUAGE OF HAPPINESS

In Bhutanese Dzongkha, the word for "happy" is *semgha (SEHM-gah).*

A HAPPY PROGNOSIS

A woman's focus on being healed leads to increased health and happiness.

Tous les jours, à tous points de vue, je vais de mieux en mieux.
("Every day, in every way, I'm getting better and better.")
—Émile Coué

Chris Frasco, age fifty-seven, sat on the doctor's exam table, her legs dangling. The paper beneath her made a crinkling sound as Chris periodically shifted her weight. At any moment, the doctor would enter, and, with luck, she would know why she had been sick for so long.

It had all started eleven months before, in January 2007. Chris had developed flu-like symptoms, including swollen glands. Her doctor had prescribed antibiotics, and Chris got better. But she still had a persistent pain in her ribs whenever she breathed and especially when she coughed. The pain had increased in severity a little every day until it became excruciating.

The doctor had treated Chris for pneumonia and pleurisy, and she had been able to get through the winter holidays. As the New Year dawned, however, Chris had found herself in severe pain. Her doctor scheduled a CAT scan and a blood screening. Chris was used to being referred for blood analysis because for more than a decade small abnormalities in her white blood cell count had surfaced from time to time, although nothing problematic had ever been diagnosed.

Chris stared at the closed exam room door for so long that she was actually startled when she heard two quick knocks. Without waiting for a response, the doctor entered carrying a file containing Chris's results.

After a quick greeting, the doctor wheeled a polished chrome stool up toward the exam table, sat down, and opened the file.

Chris felt certain that this doctor, like several previous, would inform her that her white blood cell count was "a little low" but "was within acceptable norms." Instead, he said something very different.

"I didn't call you in this morning to discuss your blood test," the doctor explained. "You are here because the CAT scan shows lesions on your bones."

Then, the doctor began to use words like *cancer* and *chemotherapy*.

This sounds serious—very serious, Chris thought.

"There are three things it might be—and there are treatments for all of them." The doctor went on to list the possible illnesses, but most of what he said was white noise to Chris. Chris selected one word as her focal point from among the hundreds the doctor spoke: *treatment*.

If there is a treatment, Chris thought to herself, *then whatever it is can be treated, and I'll be okay.*

"We're going to do a bone marrow aspiration," the doctor said, pulling out his pen and jotting a few notes in Chris's chart. "Do you know what that is? It's where we drill a hole into . . ."

"Into a person's hip," Chris said, finishing the doctor's sentence, "and then extract marrow from the core of the bone." Chris had been with her mother as she underwent a bone marrow aspiration. Her mother had found the procedure extremely painful.

"When?" Chris asked, her voice flat from shock.

"Now," the doctor said, closing the file and standing up. He bent down and wheeled the chrome stool out of the way.

Chris felt numb. That morning, she had told her husband, Dennis, that she was going to the doctor to receive the results of some tests. Her comment had barely registered with him. He had heard her say those very words a half-dozen times previously during their thirty-plus years of marriage.

Chris endured the procedure, and then drove herself home. That night she told Dennis, and the two of them cried. Chris saw for the first time what many people who develop a serious health challenge discover: it's often the person who is sick who must be strong for everyone else. Rather than feeling saddened by this realization, Chris was inspired.

When the news came back, it wasn't good. Chris had multiple myeloma—cancer of the blood. The doctor laid out a treatment plan.

There was that word again, thought Chris: *treatment*. And again she reminded herself that if there is a treatment, then there is hope.

"There's no cure," the doctor said. "But there are many people living with the disease long-term."

Chris and Dennis assembled their adult children to inform them of Chris's illness. As soon as everyone was told and the initial wave of shock and tears had lessened, three out of four of the children reached for their smartphones.

"Hold it, hold it, hold it!" Chris exclaimed, waving her hands in the air.

The three continued to thumb the keypads of their phones; one was texting, another e-mailing, and the third was placing a call.

Chris used the authoritative tone reserved for the one true power in any home—mother. "*I'm serious,*" Chris said.

These three adults, all of whom were in their thirties and had successful careers in the same field—pharmaceutical sales—seemed very young as they put away their phones and began to appeal to their mother.

"But Mom, I know a doctor who . . ."

"I've got a good friend who pioneered the treatment of . . ."

"Mom, the doctor I know interned at . . ."

"Talk to anyone you want," Chris said, continuing in a tone befitting a matriarch. "But I don't want to hear anything about how sick I'm going to get or how bad this might be."

Chris stared each of her children, in turn, in the eye as she continued. "Or the mortality rate of this disease, or the pain and side effects that go along with some treatments. I don't want to hear about other people who have had this—unless they are doing great! I don't want to hear *anything* other than conversations about me getting well."

No one spoke.

"Get it?" Chris asked.

"Yes, Mom," they all said, seeming even younger than before.

That was six years ago. Today, Chris is alive and active. Coping with cancer has been an ongoing challenge, but thus far she remains in remission and has every intention of continuing this streak.

So far, she has had four bone marrow aspirations, two stem cell transplants, and several rounds of chemo. Throughout it all, Chris continues to exude both strength and happiness.

Chris shares these three secrets for becoming happier.

1. **Read and listen to positive things—no negative news:** Chris wanted her children to understand this early. So, when they were all still quite young, she bribed them with ice cream to sit down and listen to a recording from author and motivational speaker Zig Ziglar. The three children reluctantly complied.

   A few weeks later, Chris received a call from her youngest daughter Mandy's fifth-grade teacher. "I want to talk to you about what Mandy brought for show-and-tell today," the teacher said.

   Chris held her breath, but it all came rushing out in laughter when the teacher explained, "Mandy brought in a Zig Ziglar recording. The whole class listened—it was great."

2. **Know why you're here:** Happy people have a reason for living—a purpose. You get to discern your purpose and no one other than you has to agree with or even know about your decision. Your purpose is exclusively yours; everyone has a purpose.

   "My purpose in life is to have fun every day," Chris says.

3. **Clean up your backyard:** We see all too clearly what we think others need to work on, but we are blind to our own shortcomings.

   "Take a look at who is upsetting you and why," Chris advises. "If you find someone's behavior irritating, it's often an indication that you have a propensity to act that way yourself."

"Stop focusing on how you think other people need to be different. Clean up your own backyard by working on the only person you can change—yourself."

HAPPY TO BE OF SERVICE

International Myeloma Foundation: www.myeloma.org

MY ONE TRUE HAPPINESS

A couple shares their life and their love all the way from the sixth grade to happily ever after.

Love knows not its own depth until the hour of separation.
—Kahlil Gibran

Dohrman! Votava! Toye!" The company clerk continued to rapidly call out the names of soldiers who were to come forward and receive mail from home.

Jim Redmond stood listening intently for his name. Many times during mail call, the clerk would shout Jim's name as many as twenty or even thirty times. Jim would slip through the herd of men and pick up a letter addressed in the same delicate handwriting as all the previous ones.

Whenever Jim received that many letters at once, he would be so excited that he barely noticed the wolf whistles and leering grins from some soldiers, or the silent, envious glares from others.

Jim had landed on the beach at Normandy the day after D-day. He worked as part of a mobile antiaircraft unit, providing support wherever it was needed. Jim's unit was all over the area, typically staying in one location for only a day or so. Because Jim and his buddies were constantly being moved about, mail often took longer to reach them.

So far this day, Jim had not been called to come forward and pick up a single letter.

As he waited, Jim could hear a buddy softly whistling a popular tune. Jim knew the melody and could hear the lyrics in his head as the other soldier whistled. In this song, made popular by Glenn Miller and the Andrews Sisters, a soldier begs his sweetheart not to sit under the apple tree with anyone else until he comes home from war.

Jim noted that the soldier stood with one hand held behind his back. Jim leaned in to see what the man was doing with his hidden hand. Jim noticed that his fingers were crossed for luck as he waited for a letter from his girl while whistling a please-don't-break-my-heart-while-I'm-off-serving-our-country song.

That same soldier had walked to mail call alongside Jim, complaining that he hadn't received a letter from his sweetheart in two months. "That's how it starts," the soldier had warned. "You get letters all the time, and then without warning, they stop.

"Then," the man had said heavily, "then after a while you get the letter no guy wants to receive. The maybe-we-should-take-a-break letter. Or the I-think-we're-just-meant-to-be-friends letter. Or the more honest but no less painful I've-met-someone-else letter."

Now, this same soldier stood on tiptoes, craning his neck forward as if to will the company clerk to call his name. Jim thought of the woman in the song and wondered whether she had heeded her boyfriend's plea not to sit under the apple tree with anyone else. He sighed a deep, heavy sigh.

Suddenly, the clerk grabbed the mailbag from the bottom and inverted it, giving it a stout shake. Finding the bag empty, the clerk moved on to his next task without comment.

Similarly without comment, Jim and the other soldier turned and walked back to their assigned duties. Jim smiled as he walked. *No letters today means more letters tomorrow*, he thought to himself. Jim had gone days—even weeks—without letters, but he knew that Mary Ann would remember her promise and write him every day he was away.

Jim noticed that the soldier who had stood beside him was now walking just a few feet ahead. The man stared at the ground still singing the song quietly—his voice now had an entreating quality.

I hope that guy gets a letter tomorrow, Jim thought as he wound his way back to his post.

He was now rounding day number 112 of his tour of Normandy, and Jim had seen it hundreds of times since he'd landed. A soldier would get a letter and open it with great anticipation only to learn that his love had abandoned him and now he was alone—alone among thousands of men to deal with his grief while trying to stay sharp to protect his own life, as well as the lives of his fellow soldiers.

Jim's smile widened as he realized that he had never—not once—been afraid of receiving a Dear John letter from Mary Ann. They were meant to be together. He knew it. She knew it. And come what may, their love would endure.

As for the other soldier, Jim never saw him again. He often wondered if the man ever received a love letter from his girl.

Jim, on the other hand, had received more than twelve hundred letters—one for every day he was overseas.

Jim and Mary Ann had met in Louisville, Kentucky, in 1937. That was the year of the big flood that destroyed Jim's parents' home. The Redmonds moved across town, and Jim started the sixth grade in a new school.

The first day of classes, Jim managed to find his locker, and as he fumbled with the combination, the voice of an angel caught his ear. "You must be my new neighbor," the angel said, and Jim turned to behold the most strikingly beautiful creature he had ever seen.

That day, a spark ignited a flame in both of their young souls. Jim and Mary Ann were in love from the day they met at the age of twelve until Mary Ann died. All total, they were together for seventy-four years and married for sixty-two.

Much of human happiness is determined by how well a person is able to sustain and nurture important relationships. Jim managed to be part of a happy romance with his beloved for more than six decades.

Jim is now eighty-nine. He golfs three days a week and travels the world for extended periods. He misses Mary Ann, but he remains happy and grateful to have shared so much of his life with his one true love.

Take a lesson from a truly happy husband as Jim offers three suggestions for happier relationships.

1. **Tell the truth:** The foundation of any relationship is trust, and we trust those we know will be honest with us. "Too many men have relationships that fall apart due to a lack of honesty," Jim says. "If you share your life with someone, they deserve to know that they can trust you to tell the truth."

2. **An investment in family pays the highest dividends:** Jim and Mary Ann raised three children while Jim was busy building his career as an architect, but he was always available to work through difficulties with his wife and children whenever they arose.

    "If there was a problem," Jim says, "we stayed with it until we reached a satisfactory solution. As a result, the kids were happy. And because the kids were happy, there was less stress on our marriage, so we were happy."

3. **Stay positive:** Jim says, "There were many times when my wife and I had challenges. We would wonder how we'd ever get through something, and then there would always be a tomorrow when things were better."

    "Keeping your attitude up even when things are tough creates a fertile field for happiness."

Occasionally Jim pulls out the letters Mary Ann wrote to him during World War II. They are paper and ink portals that take him back to his days apart from her for the first time. As he reads through the letters again, they ease Jim's wait until he's again in his Mary Ann's arms.

Jim knows that when he and Mary Ann are at last reunited, there will be no more breaks in their *happily ever after.*

CROWN ME HAPPY

A young beauty queen overcomes significant challenges to make her life and the lives of others happier.

There is no cosmetic for beauty like happiness.
—Marguerite Gardiner, Countess of Blessington

"Did you hear that?" twelve-year-old Demi King asked her mother, Pattie, in a whisper.

"I sure did," Pattie replied empathetically.

"She's type 1 diabetic just like me, and she *just* found out—like, a week ago," said Demi.

"Yes, I heard."

"Can you imagine being told that right before something this stressful?"

"It would be hard. But she seems to be handling it okay—so far."

"I'm going to go talk to her."

Without another word, Demi rose and walked toward the girl who was departing backstage. Technically, she was Demi's competition for the title of National American Miss, but Demi never thought about the other girls that way.

They were kids just like her. Sure, someone would win and the rest would not, but Demi believes that pageants are supposed to be fun. And according to her, it's fun being nice to people.

During the rehearsal for the interview segment, the little girl had disclosed that she was recently diagnosed with type 1 diabetes. In another contest with a different group of girls, one of the challengers might have exploited such vulnerability behind the scenes in an attempt to win.

But not here.

The National American Miss contest is not a place for Honey Boo Boo types. Here, the girls are just as they appear. They do not wear makeup or outlandish gowns, nor do they wear wigs or pile their hair atop their heads. The girls do not wear flippers to remove gaps between their teeth and make them appear larger and more dazzling.

National American Miss celebrates authentic beauty—and Demi's beautiful face is matched by an equally beautiful heart.

"You're so pretty," Demi said to the girl as she caught up with her backstage.

"Thank you," she replied. "So are *you*."

Demi smiled, and the two gazed at each other for a second.

"I'm type 1, too," Demi said.

"*Really?*" exclaimed the other girl. "When did you find out?"

"Nine years ago," she replied.

The girl took a nearly imperceptible half step back to widen her view of Demi in order to survey her more fully.

"*You* look okay," she said softly, without considering how her words might be received.

"Me? I'm great!" said Demi. "My mom owns a dance studio, and I dance all the time. I get to do pageants and make new friends. Life is *awesome*."

The other girl gave Demi a quizzical, almost pouting, look. Demi smiled warmly and reached out to gently squeeze her shoulder.

"It's going to be okay," Demi said. "You'll see."

The girl looked beseechingly into Demi's eyes. Demi continued to smile and gave the girl a little nod before they parted. As the pageant unfolded over the next three days, this girl watched Demi closely. By her estimation, Demi certainly did appear to be "great."

Three days later, when all of the splendor and fun of the pageant faded and Demi departed for home, taking with her more awards and acknowledgments than any other contestant, the other little girl went home with something far more valuable than ribbons and trophies. Thanks to Demi, she went home with *hope*.

To say that Demi is a happy preteen is to state the patently obvious. She beams with joy. Demi's sweetness, as well as her effusively happy nature, makes her unique when compared to most teenage girls.

However, this is just where Demi's uniqueness begins. Consider her ultimate idol for a preteen: "Most girls my age are into One Direction and Justin Bieber, but for me—there's only Donald Trump."

Seriously. This burgeoning adolescent girl's favorite celebrity is The Donald. In Demi's bedroom, you will find both a photo of Trump with Demi's smiling face photoshopped in beside his and a life-size cardboard cutout of Donald Trump.

When you learn Demi's next major goal, you begin to understand this twelve-year-old girl's fascination with Donald Trump. "My dream is to be Miss Universe," Demi says matter-of-factly. "Donald Trump owns the rights to Miss Universe. So, I'll meet him when I win."

The other reason Demi loves Trump: "He's just so *cool*—you know? He sees what he wants, and he goes for it."

From the time she was born—even before she was aware of it—Demi has also been going for it.

The doctors gave Demi less than a year to survive. She had been born with no immune system whatsoever. Her body did not produce any natural barriers or treatments for the myriad viruses and diseases that assault human beings—especially children.

Medically, it's called severe combined immunodeficiency syndrome (SCIDS), although most people know it as the bubble-boy disease, referring to the 1976 made-for-TV movie *The Boy in the Plastic Bubble*, which starred John Travolta.

As Demi reached four months, she slipped into a coma. The doctors estimated she had only a few months to live—even on life support. With no immune system, a simple cold could kill her.

Then a radical new treatment was attempted. Demi received an immune system transplant.

Stem cells were harvested from an umbilical cord donated five years earlier by a new mother. The cells were then implanted into Demi's tiny little body, where they lay dormant, ready to take on whatever form was required. The doctors blasted little Demi with chemotherapy, igniting the stem cells to rise up and protect her, thereby creating an immune system.

The procedure was a complete success. However, the chemo caused Demi's pancreas to shut down, leaving her a diabetic. She not only pricks her finger five times a day to monitor her blood sugar and gives herself regular insulin injections, but she also has two needles that remain in her body constantly.

"I've got two needles in my butt—one in each cheek," Demi says with a big smile. "You can't really see them except when I'm dancing, and you see them under my leotard."

Demi has overcome her struggles to live a life that is very happy. Here are her three tips for happiness.

1. **Help others feel happy:** The little girl Demi offered encouragement to at the pageant is just one of many examples of Demi reaching out to help others feel happy.

    Demi has created a program at the children's hospital where she receives treatment. Children who are diagnosed with diabetes are given a teddy bear and a handwritten note of assurance and encouragement from Demi. So far, she has given away more than five hundred bears.

2. **Keep your spirits up:** Like other happy people, Demi reminds us that keeping ourselves happy is our own responsibility. "If I ever get to feeling down," she offers, "I put on a crown and a sash from one of the pageants, and I wear it around the house until I feel better—it's kinda weird, but it works!"

3. **Be yourself:** Nothing depletes a person's happiness so much as being inauthentic. Being genuine means that you are comfortable with yourself. And a high level of self-esteem is critical to being happy.

    Demi adds, "People are unhappy because they don't like who they are, or they're trying to be someone they're not.

    "Be yourself—it's the only way to really be happy."

DIVINE HAPPINESS

A man remains happy even as he adjusts to a traumatic loss.

We deem those happy who, from the experience of life, have learned to bear its ills, without being overcome by them.
—Juvenal

You're going to get in trouble if you keep doing this," Steve warned through his perpetual smile.

The young man ignored Steve's comment as he continued to thumb through a dog-eared composition notebook. Here and there he stopped at a page and rotated the book around so that both Steve and his son, Scott, could appreciate his artwork.

"Man, that's a good one," Scott said admiringly.

"Uh-huh, yeah . . . oh, hey, check this one!" the young man said, flipping a couple of pages further.

"*Nice*," Scott said. "Dad, what do you think of that one?"

Scott's dad, Steve Lemons, was fifty-seven years old, and for a preacher who also happened to be a dad, he was pretty cool.

"I think they're all really good," he said. "You're obviously very talented."

"Yeah . . . thanks," the young man said as if distracted. He continued to flip the pages and spin the book back and forth. "It's a gift . . . I mean, I've worked hard, you know? I've been drawing all my life, but now I get to take my art and give it real permanence.

"There's a bond that's formed, you know?" he continued. "There is this blood and ink connection between the artist and the person getting a tattoo. A tattoo is forever—that's a commitment, you know?"

The young man gazed off for a moment as if reveling in the nobility of his occupation. Then, returning his focus to his notebook, he added: "And, man, if people like your stuff, they'll show it to their friends. When that happens—you're set, *everybody* will want to get inked by you."

Scott pulled up his pants leg to look at the calf his artist friend would soon decorate with a needle. He had a tattoo on both of his arms as well as on his left calf. Now he was ready to add something to his right calf as well.

"And so, you're not a *licensed* tattoo artist?" Steve asked.

"Me? No. Oh, no," the young man said. "You mean, like, state standards and all that stuff? Nah. I'm an artist, man—that's all my clients care about, you know? And because I don't have to go through all that license stuff, my prices are *way* better."

"They're nice designs," Steve said. Then, turning to Scott he added, "Well, you're thirty-two, *and* you've already got three other tattoos, so you certainly don't need my permission."

All three men laughed.

For the next twenty minutes, the young man continued to display his drawings. Meanwhile, Scott imagined his new tattoo complete, healed over, and looking *awesome*.

Steve, however, felt a distant foreboding as if having just witnessed a small crack of lightning that would soon yield earth-shattering thunder. The distance of lightning can be measured by the time it takes to hear its thunder clap. Steve wouldn't have to wait very long to hear the thunder that came with Scott's new tattoo.

Scott contracted MRSA thanks to an unsterile needle—the infection settled in his hip. MRSA, methicillin-resistant *Staphylococcus aureus,* is a rapidly growing bacterium that defies antibiotics. Treatment of MRSA is long and can be very painful.

A port was installed in Scott's body to allow for the administration of extremely high doses of antibiotics. Scott's hip was opened up surgically and doctors attempted to scrape away infected cells—a long, intense, and agonizing procedure. Scott lay in bed for weeks, swimming in a sea of pain as he tried to recover from the operation.

The good news was that Scott was recovering in the very hospital where Steve served as the chaplain supervisor. Scott's father was always close by, as were Steve's students and fellow chaplains. In addition, members of the little church Steve served on the weekends came by regularly to cheer Scott on and to pray with him.

Scott went home, but very soon a blood test showed that the infection still raged within his body. Again, he went to the hospital and again his hip was opened up while surgeons attempted to cut away any remnants of the bacteria. Both the procedure and the recovery were as painful the second time as they had been the first.

The doctors finally released Scott, and home health-care nurses visited him regularly. One day after testing Scott's blood, the nurse called Scott's doctor and his parents. "Something is seriously wrong," she said. "The infection is getting worse."

As Steve and his wife, Jennie, converged on Scott's home to accompany him to the hospital, they found their son lying in bed unmoving.

"Let's get going," Jennie urged her son.

"No," Scott said softly. "No, Mom. No more. I, I can't."

"What are you talking about, buddy?" Steve said laughing and placing a hand on his son's shoulder. "You were getting better; this is just a little setback. You're going to be fine."

"No, Dad," Scott replied. "I'm sorry. I just can't go through this again—I'd rather die." And then, looking down at the floor as if ashamed, Scott repeated, "I'm sorry."

Steve and Jennie stared at each other. Long gone were the days when they could simply order their son to do as they wanted. Besides, that had never really been their style.

From his decades of working with families in hospitals, Steve knew that the right to make decisions about one's own health care must be sacrosanct. Even if it means that the person is choosing to give up the fight to live. And even if that person is your own child.

That was October 4, 2011.

The following day, Scott was walking around the house at one in the afternoon. By four, he was gone. Scott's body had become septic, and he died less than ninety days after receiving his initial diagnosis.

The grieving process is ongoing for Steve and Jennie Lemons, but Steve is quick to point out, "I really believe I live a happy life. Even going through what I am going through, I am still happy."

The young man who tattooed Scott with the dirty needle was later arrested after another one of his clients contracted a serious infection. But Steve holds no hatred or animosity toward the man. Instead, he chooses to be happy.

He offers these three suggestions for happiness.

1. **Cultivate positive spirituality:** "I never for a moment believed that God was responsible for Scott's sickness and death," Steve says. "God gets blamed for things that simply just happen."

    As part of Steve's assessment when working with patients, he ascertains whether the person believes in a loving, nonjudgmental God or in a God that is wrathful and angry.

    "The more positive a person's view of God is," he says, "the more likely they are to get better."

2. **Never stop learning:** Steve had made a decision to go back to school to acquire a doctoral degree in pastoral care counseling. After Scott died, he debated continuing his education. Ultimately, he realized how much joy he derives from simply learning, and he opted to proceed.

    Steve says, "We should always be actively learning and growing—it keeps us interested in life; it keeps us happy."

3. **Dwell on the positive:** When Steve and Jennie talk about Scott, they don't lament the times they will miss having with their son. Rather, they focus on the good times they shared.

    "We have a lot of good memories about Scott," Steve adds. "That's what we choose to focus on."

A VISION OF HAPPINESS

A blind boy defies the odds to become a radio celebrity.

We differ, blind and seeing, one from another, not in our senses, but in the use we make of them, in the imagination and courage with which we seek wisdom beyond the senses.
—Helen Keller

Now you just close your eyes, hon. We're going to give you some gas—just like at a filling station," the nurse sang to Dan in a lilting Southern drawl.

Young as he was, Dan could have repeated the words along with her—drawl included—but he knew that would be rude. As the nurse placed the rubber anesthesia cup over Dan's small face for yet another operation on his right eye, Dan knew what was to follow.

He closed his eyes. His mind registered only a slight difference between his eyes being open or shut. A wavy feeling passed through him, and then Dan was asleep.

It was 1960, and Dan was in an operating room in Key West, Florida. This would be the fifth operation on Dan's right eye in his brief five years of life. Dan was born with congenital cataracts in both eyes and glaucoma in his right. The glaucoma was spreading to Dan's left eye, so doctors were now removing his right eye. Henceforth, he would wear a prosthetic right eye.

Dan's vision problems can be traced back to his mother contracting German measles during her third month of pregnancy with Dan. Often, infants born under such conditions are blind *and* deaf, and can also be severely mentally handicapped. Fortunately, Dan's challenges begin and end with his sight.

The doctors estimated that Dan could see only about 10 percent of what most children see. His vision would probably never get better, but if he was careful, Dan could maintain the modicum of sight he possessed.

Had young Dan been completely blind, he might have adapted better socially. Instead, he was trapped in a world between sight and darkness. The darkness was nearly complete, and the sliver of light taunted him to be more like other kids.

Dan longed to do things most boys his age took for granted, especially to play baseball like his brother, John. John could see the sadness in Dan's face as he stood beneath the shade of a sprawling water oak, his head moving slowly from side to side as if trying to catch a perfect angle that would complete his vision.

"Hey, Dan," John called, walking away from the game. "Come umpire." The other boys groaned irritably at John's invitation, but he silenced them with a glare.

Dan's heart leapt. He ambled as quickly as he dared toward his brother's voice, always careful to avoid cypress knees and errant bits of debris that might cause him to fall.

John guided his brother behind the catcher, whose rotund body would offer some protection. For the next hour and a half, the game proceeded with Dan standing in the moist Florida heat, calling balls and strikes—most of which the other boys ignored due to inaccuracy.

Whether standing impotently behind home plate or trying to relate to kids at school, Dan's unique presence caused some to feel uncomfortable, and many found it easier to discount him. As he grew older, he withdrew into himself. He rarely spoke to others unless they initiated the interaction. Dan soon became accustomed to receding in the background in most social situations.

Dan rarely spoke—but when he did, it was with a painfully awkward stammer. His words would stream through his mind as clearly as the scrolling lights along buildings in Times Square. Unfortunately, they flew too fast for Dan's mouth—which would find itself still forming the beginning of soft consonants long after other people had picked up the conversation to spare Dan embarrassment.

Dan was almost totally blind, and to those who didn't know him, he sounded as if he was mentally retarded. Dan's doctors recommended that he be placed into a home for the blind. There, he would at least learn a skill—such as stuffing envelopes—that he could do for the rest of his life.

To their credit, Dan's parents refused to send him to a home. They did their best to find ways for Dan to fit in with the other kids at school, including retyping his reading assignments for him, using a large print typewriter.

With few friends and limitations on the activities he might pursue, Dan listened to the radio constantly. Deep in the recesses of his mind, a dream began to develop. Dan began to think about the men and women who worked at the radio station. They always seemed to be having so much fun. Being a disc jockey would be a *great* job to have someday.

Then, as if feeling sheepish for daring to dream so big, Dan said aloud: "Yeah, good l . . . lu . . . l . . . lu . . . lu . . . *luck!*"

Dan didn't know what the inside of a radio station looked like. For that matter, he barely knew what the inside of his home looked like. But, after he turned off his radio late at night, he imagined himself there—actually there—at a real radio station. *Wouldn't that be something?* he thought to himself.

In his solitude, Dan not only listened to the great radio announcers of the day, but he began to mimic them as well. As a young teen, Dan would cup his right hand over his ear to better capture the sound of his voice, and then repeat the weather forecast, report sports scores, and pretend to interview celebrities.

Then Dan made an interesting discovery. If he could get people to laugh, he could get their attention and approval in a nonthreatening way. Dan went from class outcast to class clown.

Dan finished high school and went to college, where he nearly failed his freshman year because he was always at the campus radio station. He learned to read radio copy by wearing both contacts *and* thick glasses, and then sliding the printed paper up his left cheek as he read—the text only millimeters from his eye. And yet with all the machinations it took for Dan to read on the radio, he managed to sound ad-libbed, genial, and often very funny.

Today, blind-boy Dan—stammering, uncertain Dan, whose destiny seemed to be life in a sweatshop for the blind—is the program director, operations manager, and primary voice talent for KIXI in Seattle, Washington, the fourteenth largest radio market in the United States.

Dan is happily married, and he and his bride, June, have seen the world together. Dan has done things many fully sighted people only dream of doing, including rafting in the Grand Canyon, hiking through the Amazon Rain Forest, and exploring the Great Pyramid of Giza. According to him and those who know him, Dan is a very happy guy.

In that melodious voice that is equal parts sunshine and honey, Dan offers these three tips for happiness.

1. **Spend your life enriching other people's lives:** "My job is to make people's lives a little more enjoyable. If they're having a bad day, maybe I can make them laugh and play them music so they feel better. I'm happy when I can see that other people are happy, based on something I've done," Dan says.

2. **Laugh often:** Dan finds that laughter builds bridges between people. "Sometimes, when people meet me they feel a little uncomfortable, so I like to give them a big smile and identify the elephant in the room so we can both laugh. I'll say, 'Hey, you *may* have noticed I have a sight problem.' After we laugh, and they see I'm cool with how I am, they relax."

3. **Find your smile:** When Dan was sixteen, he toured WNBC in New York City. "I got to see the famous Ted Brown do his show. After that, I couldn't stop smiling. I had found what makes me happy, and now I do it for a living. I found my smile.

   "I believe *everyone* has something that makes them smile that they can also do to make money and serve others."

HAPPY TO BE OF SERVICE

American Foundation for the Blind: www.AFB.org

GROWING IN HAPPINESS

The burst of the housing bubble doesn't diminish a real estate developer's happiness.

What does not kill me makes me stronger.
—Friedrich Nietzsche

J ohn Galarde stretched his tall, muscular frame out on a weight bench at his local gym. He wriggled his body up the bench so that his chest lay directly beneath the heavy barbell.

John let his elbows drop gradually toward the floor, stretching his chest muscles. He took a deep breath. As he exhaled, he crossed his arms over his torso and closed his eyes.

In his mind, he was thirty years younger. John stood on a wooden stage beneath the harsh glare from dozens of spotlights. Hundreds of fans urged him and the other competitors on with their screams. In the balance was the 1983 Mr. North Carolina title.

John fast-forwarded through his mental playback to the announcement of the winner. As the announcer proclaimed the new champion, John heard his own name, and it rang like a shot in his ears. After years of training, he had been named the top bodybuilder in the state.

John savored the feelings of that long-ago victory for another moment. He felt a surge of confidence and an explosion of energy. He opened his eyes and reached his hands up to the heavy bar. He took one deep breath and, without further hesitation, pressed the weight upward and lifted it off its cradle. John executed a perfect set of bench presses, and then nestled the bar safely back in the rack.

John stood and constricted his pectoral muscles tightly, increasing blood flow to his chest and extracting the nitric acid that burned within his pecs. John looked at himself in the mirror. As much as his body has grown through weight lifting, his mind and spirit have grown and developed by facing life's weighty challenges.

In 2006, John was on his way up. He was married with three children. He had gone from selling real estate to developing neighborhoods and building homes. And business was booming.

John lives in North Carolina's New Hanover County—a serene and beautiful location bordered on the east by the white sands and deep green waters of the Atlantic Ocean and on the west by historic Wilmington and the majestic Cape Fear River.

In a single year, land values in New Hanover County more than doubled, with the price of the average lot going from $50,000 to nearly $125,000.

John was at the proverbial right place at the right time. He was developing three hundred homes on land secured with a loan from the bank. John's investment was never in doubt because within a few short months of his offering the parcels for sale, he had nearly half of them under contract. His net worth soared to $11 million.

Plans were drawn up to have roads built and sewers run into his developments. However, the work couldn't begin because county officials placed a one-year ban on sewer construction. All John could do was sit and wait for the calendar pages to slowly flip by.

During his twelve-month wait, he prepared himself for the bustle of activity that would soon commence. He hired additional staff and purchased equipment. When the sewer moratorium was lifted, John would be prepared to burst out of the gate and build, build, build.

"And then the housing market died," John says, shaking his head and smiling warmly. "We had contracts with builders at an average price of $115,000 per lot. Twelve months later—boom! The appraised value of the lots dropped sixty-five percent! I had 125 contracts," John sighs, "And they all fell through—every single one."

The bank foreclosed on John's land. He had no choice but to lay off his entire staff of thirty-five people. He cancelled business deals with all of his subcontractors. In total, more than three hundred people were out of work from the shock wave that had hit John.

As the housing market continued to decline, John scrambled to keep things together. Then, an attorney with the Securities and Exchange Commission called to ask if he had ever heard the name *Madoff*.

That name soon made national headlines. Former NASDAQ chairman Bernie Madoff created and managed a Ponzi scheme of epic proportions that had masqueraded as a legitimate and prof-itable hedge fund.

Prior to the housing collapse, John had managed to save up money well into seven figures. Madoff made off with every cent John had, as well as billions of dollars that he swindled from people just like John.

John and his family went from living in a 4,500-square-foot house on the water to being homeless. The house, the boat, the cars, the wave runners, the jewelry—everything—was liqui-dated. They found themselves making regular trips to the local consignment store to sell whatever clothes remained. For an entire summer, they bounced from relative to relative.

John felt like he was under a weight that threatened to crush him at any moment.

After losing everything, John became seriously ill for a time, with twin blood clots in his leg and a severe staph infection in his knee. And yet, through it all he remained happy. Regardless of the weight life piled on him, he resolved to one day prevail, and he kept his spirits up.

Here are John's three tips to being happy amid adversity.

1. **Exercise—for your mind as well as your body:** John offers, "Athletes are successful in other areas of their life because of the mental training it takes to develop their bodies. You can-not get under a heavy barbell and not be there mentally—it'll crush you. You have to be there in your head, first, and in your body, second."

    Regular exercise makes you mentally strong and gives you physical and emotional energy. It is a primary ingredient for happiness.

2. **Accept what comes your way:** "When you go through upheavals, it's going to do one of two things," John observes.

"It's going to make you wiser or it's going to make you bitter—and it's up to you to choose between the two.

"Wisdom comes from accepting things you can't change," John says, paraphrasing a famous prayer. "It doesn't mean you give up. You still have hope that things can change, you just let go of your insistence that things be different—they are what they are and that's that."

3. **Selectively relive the past:** When things get tough, John closes his eyes and calls to mind previous successes and happy experiences. He amplifies these feelings in his mind until he feels them completely.

   "This is the express train to happiness," John says. "The morning after my son won a big football game, he told me he woke up feeling *great*. So I told him to remember that feeling and bring it up whenever he gets down."

   John shrugs his big shoulders, "Most people replay the bad stuff that's happened in the past—that's not going to make you feel better."

   "Instead, reach out for the good feelings. Think back to your first kiss, a big win at sports, falling in love, the birth of a child—it doesn't matter so long as it makes you feel really good.

   "It's not easy to force yourself to do this when you're low—when the weight of the world is on top of you. But just like weight lifting, if you can get your mind into the game first, your body can make it happen!"

John is starting over and is where he was twenty years ago in real estate sales. As to the future—time will tell. John still has dreams and the stamina to succeed.

Whether he becomes a deca-millionaire again is irrelevant to John. He has the one thing money can't buy: happiness.

HAPPY TAILS TO YOU

A very special hospice volunteer brings joy to patients and their families.

That last day does not bring extinction to us, but change of place.
—Marcus Tullius Cicero

P reston stopped to greet the volunteers who staffed the welcome desk at the nursing home. Everyone smiled at Preston, and he smiled back. He then turned and walked up the main hall. He had been here hundreds of times and knew the place well.

As he walked, his head swept from side to side. Here and there Preston noticed familiar faces, familiar sights, and, especially, familiar smells.

Preston was a retired athlete now volunteering at a nursing home as well as at a hospice center. Primarily, he works with patients near death, but the purpose of his visit this day was simply to go from room to room and offer love and encouragement to the patients.

Preston loved doing this.

Ahead, Preston saw a young man hunched over in a wheelchair. He appeared to be asleep. The man's middle-aged mother pushed his chair unhurriedly up the hall.

Preston had never seen the man before but walked his way and stood before him. His mother greeted Preston, and the young man, who seemed to be blind, reached out. As he touched Preston's ear, a smile spread across his lifeless face.

"Skipper?" the young man asked dreamily.

His mother was shocked to hear her son's voice. She leaned over and waited for him to speak again. Her son ran his hand down Preston's face and rubbed his chin.

To no one's surprise, Preston reached out his tongue, licked the man's hand, and then wagged his tail happily.

Preston is fawn colored and quite large for a racing dog, weighing nearly one hundred pounds. Judy Gauron and her husband, Karl, adopted him from a greyhound rescue center when he was five years old. He was over-the-hill by racing standards.

Preston now regularly went with Judy to bring a loving connection to people who are either near death or severely incapacitated.

As the young man stroked Preston's strong neck, he once more called out the name of his own boyhood dog: "Skipper? Good boy, Skipper, that's a good boy." Preston used his nose to scoop the man's hand back up to his ears; he loved having his ears rubbed.

The man's mother began to cry as she leaned forward and scrubbed Preston's furry head. After a moment, she hugged her son, wiped her eyes, and resumed pushing the wheelchair slowly up the hall.

The young man never opened his eyes again. He passed away that night. His final conscious connection had been unconditional love from Preston.

Judy's work with the hospice began when she volunteered to do administrative work. She loves the hospice's mission and believes that every person should have someone to love and support them as they transition from this life to their next stage of existence—whatever that is.

Judy decided to personalize her contribution to the hospice by working directly with those under its care. She found the idea both appealing and a little frightening. Preston became a bridge for Judy. When she heard about programs that certify dogs to visit care facilities, Judy took Preston to be approved.

"He passed with flying colors," says Judy. "His calm demeanor made Preston a great fit, and he was able to obey all the required commands—except one."

Like all greyhounds that were bred and raised to run at the track, Preston could not obey the command *sit*. The intense training of young greyhound puppies overdevelops their legs so that as adults they can either stand or lie down—but they can't sit.

As Judy began to make rounds and work with patients, she noticed how people opened up whenever a dog was present. Very few people dislike dogs, and for those who love them, they are an instant connection with one's own childhood. Stoic adults will soften and become childlike in the presence of a dog.

The love of dogs is a common bond that unites people. Judy experiences a great deal of happiness taking Preston to meet patients and their families at the care center, and she feels high as a kite after their visits.

"But isn't working with all those sick, dying people depressing?" friends often ask.

"Actually, it's the exact opposite," Judy says. "Being with someone who is dying is a privilege. I get tremendous satisfaction, and I love doing something that improves the quality of people's lives."

Judy is a truly happy person. She has found that the following three things contribute to happiness.

1. **Practice compassion:** "I think there is a correlation between compassion and happiness," Judy says. "When you're with someone in pain, it's like you can feel it. You want so much for that person to be happy that, somehow, you—yourself—begin to feel happier."

   "I know that when we enter a patient's room, it's Preston they really want to see," Judy says. "But I get to be part of this and it's priceless."

2. **Nurture what makes you happy:** When something brings you joy, focus on it and seek to extend the feeling. All too often, people focus on what's wrong or what they fear so much that they let the good experiences go barely noticed.

   "Becoming a person who focuses on the good things takes effort," Judy says. "It doesn't just happen. But when you work at it long enough, it becomes a habit—a habit of being happy."

3. **Do something you're passionate about:** "If you love to quilt—quilt," Judy says. "So many people either don't invest time trying to figure out what they love, or, if they know, they still don't spend time doing what makes them happy.

   "Everybody has something that makes them feel good. For me, it's working with people who are making their life's transition. What's yours?"

After five and a half years of generous, loving service, Preston developed a limp. Greyhounds are prone to bone cancer and an

X-ray confirmed that the disease had ravaged his hip. Judy could see the pain in his eyes whenever he tried to walk.

When pain pills and steroids did nothing to lesson his pain, Judy and Karl made the decision to let Preston go. They made an arrangement with the veterinarian to come to their home. Preston would be given the same loving care a hospice patient would receive.

After Preston was given a drug to calm him down, he was wrapped in a blanket and placed in front of a warm fireplace. Judy and Karl petted and kissed him. Ambient music played in the background as the couple affirmed their love for their departing friend.

When they were ready, the doctor gave Preston the injection. Judy and Karl held each other as they both mourned and celebrated the life of this amazing dog.

Perhaps there's a heaven. If so, there were hundreds of old friends waiting on Preston. He had been there for them as they left their earthly lives, and now they welcomed him to his next life. And perhaps, just perhaps, Preston is there right now, wagging his tail and waiting for us to join him.

HAPPY REPORTING

A television reporter shares happiness with her viewers—and they love her for it.

I shall take the heart . . . for brains do not make one happy, and happiness is the best thing in the world.
—L. Frank Baum, line spoken by the Tin Man
in *The Wonderful Wizard of Oz* (1900)

"C ould have been worse, right Kathy?" the local news anchor scoffed as Kathy Quinn entered the broadcast studio.

"Absolutely!" Kathy responded with a smile that outshone the stage lights overhead. "We could have had *twenty* inches of snow instead of only thirteen!" she exclaimed as she walked toward her colleague.

"It's actually a beautiful morning," Kathy continued as she reached forward and deftly straightened the man's tie. "Everything is so quiet, and the way the streetlights refract off the snow . . ."

The irritated groans of several of the crew could be heard coming from various parts of the studio. The anchor leaned forward and looked searchingly into Kathy's eyes. "Are you for real?" he asked.

Kathy's smile grew even larger. "If you're a *Negative Nancy*, I'm not talking to you today."

She pulled the man's suit jacket snug in front of the tie, which now hung perfectly. "But," she added with a grin, "if you're a *Positive Patty*, I'll talk to you."

The anchor gave Kathy a brief nod of thanks for straightening his tie. "Are you going to be talking about how *great* and *beautiful* and *wonderful* and *awesome* this snowstorm is?" he asked, grabbing the first segment's copy and turning to walk toward the news desk.

"Absolutely!" Kathy responded with a broad smile.

"I'll pass, thanks," he said with a dismissive wave.

"Suit yourself!" Kathy chirped.

An associate producer hustled past, barking orders into a cell phone. Kathy caught the young woman's eye and grinned. The woman returned Kathy's smile, then, shaking her head as if released from a dream, resumed her frantic conversation.

Glancing at the clock on the wall, Kathy noticed that it was 4:17 a.m. The smell of fresh coffee wafted through the building spread by the massive air-conditioning system that kept the crew comfortable under the harsh lights. The television station buzzed with activity. People darted this way and that way, stepping gingerly over shifting snarls of camera cables.

Kathy unzipped her heavy parka that bore the station's logo. She slid her animal print scarf off her shoulders and poured herself a cup of coffee. Kathy warmed her hands on the sides of the mug and deeply inhaled its hypnotic aroma. The coffee and Kathy's eyes were the same color—and both were equally warm.

Primarily, Kathy reported features and special events at this particular station. That morning, the special event was an arctic blast that had dumped thirteen inches of snow in just over fifteen hours.

Kathy gazed around the station once more to make certain she had greeted everyone. Seeing the first task of her day now complete, Kathy walked into the assignment office.

"Okay," she said. "*Let's do it.*" Kathy grabbed the clipboard containing her recommended shots for the morning, checked in with the show's producer, put her scarf and coat back on, and stepped out into the lit parking lot.

Kathy inhaled deeply—the air was so cold that each breath felt constricted in her throat. "Exhilarating!" Kathy proclaimed as she slid into the TV station's remote broadcast van idling in the parking lot. The van's windshield wipers slapped rhythmically from side to side with a loud *shloosh, shloosh* sound.

Kathy's cameraman was in the driver's seat next to her; he had been warming the van while waiting for her. As she closed her door, he stopped texting, donned his gloves, and reached to snap his seat belt in place. "Good morning, Kathy," he said, still groggy from sleep.

"Yes it is," Kathy said effusively. And, with that, she was off to report about downed power lines, traffic pileups, airline cancellations, and anything else related to the storm. And she did it with a genuine smile on her face.

Every television station wants to have its very own Kathy Quinn—its own personal ray of sunshine.

Many stations hire someone to fill the role of happy counterpoint to the negativity of most news stories. Regardless of the reporter's talent, if he or she isn't genuinely upbeat, the stories fall flat.

Kathy, who now reports for WDAF Channel 4 in Kansas City, Missouri, is the real deal. She has the talent to cover a story, and the genuine, effervescent smile to entice you to watch. She seems like a friend or, at the very least, a friendly person—because she is.

Kathy doesn't report "positive" news exclusively. But, somehow, she finds a way to put a positive spin on nearly every story she reports.

In 2002, Kathy was contacted by several people informing her that a sex abuse scandal involving a local priest was about to come to light. She was asked to break the story to her viewers. Kathy is a devoted Catholic and sharing the story troubled her.

However, as she talked to the people involved, Kathy discovered that the young boys who had been molested were now all grown men—and Kathy happened to know many of them. As she delved into the story, she heard about the anguish, pain, and embarrassment each of them felt.

"I helped those men bring their story to light," she says. "Now they can get help. Many of them had never told anybody about what had happened. It was very therapeutic for them to share and get support from one another. I broke the story, but it didn't break my faith."

Many news reporters burn out. The constant emotional drain of reporting on violence, rape, murder, natural disasters, corruption, and disease eats at their souls until they throw up their hands and walk away.

But not Kathy.

Kathy has found a way to use her medium not only to inform viewers as to what is happening but also to celebrate and magnify what's good. Kathy hosts a regular segment called *Pay It Forward*, where people are invited to nominate a person who has unselfishly given to others. Kathy weaves a story honoring the benevolent person and then presents him or her with $300.

"It's not a lot," Kathy admits. "But it lets us publicly thank those who are making our city better."

As to how to become happy like Kathy, she offers these three suggestions.

1. **Be timeless:** Whenever she is asked her age, Kathy always responds, "I'm timeless.

   "People are so caught up in their age," she says. "*You* decide how old you are, not the calendar."

   When Kathy tried out for a part in the movie *Mr. and Mrs. Bridge*, starring Paul Newman and Joanne Woodward, the casting director asked her, "How old are you?"

   Without hesitation, Kathy responded confidently, "How old do you want me to be?"

   Kathy got the part.

2. **Smile and listen:** "One of my grandmothers was Irish and the other was Mexican," Kathy says. "They had a great friendship even though they didn't speak each other's language. Why? Because they smiled and listened to one another."

3. **When you fall, get up quickly:** "You're not normal if you don't get down," Kathy says. "But as soon as I find that I'm getting a little low, I start listing aloud all the things I'm grateful for—this works every time."

A HAPPY
HOMECOMING

A truly special young woman inspires happiness in her classmates as well as in her city.

Aerodynamically, the bumblebee shouldn't be able to fly, but the bumblebee doesn't know that, so it goes on flying anyway.
—Mary Kay Ash

Allyssa Brubeck slid out of her cheerleading uniform and hastily donned the dress specially chosen for this very important occasion.

Cindy, Allyssa's mom, slid the long zipper up the back of her gown, stepped back, and smiled proudly. The sounds of a hotly contested high school football game could be heard through the concrete walls of the girls' locker room where they stood.

"Are you nervous?" Cindy asked.

"I'm fine," Allyssa said, smiling. The two embraced for a long moment. Then, gripping each other tightly by the hand, they walked toward the exit.

As they stepped out of the locker room, the sounds of screaming fans, a marching band, cheerleaders, and the stadium announcer reverberated together, creating a din of pure excitement.

Mike, Allyssa's dad, stood waiting outside the locker room. When Allyssa and Cindy saw him, they laughed because they hadn't seen him in a suit in a very long time. Mike reached out his hands to place a corsage of delicate white flowers on his daughter's wrist; his eyes were misty with tears.

Mike kissed Allyssa's cheek, and then asked, "Are you nervous?"

"I'm fine," Allyssa said again.

The trio stood awkwardly for a moment. "Well, let's go—I guess," Mike said, and they all held hands. As they walked along the running track toward the football field, they felt the surge of the game pulsating through the structure. It seemed as if the ground itself shook with the fierce rivalry being played out.

Allyssa, Mike, and Cindy walked quickly. Little did they know that they were walking into a setup.

It had all begun weeks before and had grown steadily. Someone had posed an interesting idea, and others had picked up on it. Then it had gone viral. Students' phones were being blown up with Twitter posts about the idea.

And yet with hundreds of high school kids involved, not one single adult had any idea about this coordinated effort on the part of the students. Their secrecy had been absolute.

As Allyssa, her mom, and her dad rounded the back of the bleachers to reenter the field where Allyssa had been cheerleading during the first quarter, students began to lean down and call out Allyssa's name. One by one they got her attention and shouted out well wishes. Allyssa smiled and received the comments graciously. She stopped frequently to greet students and their families.

"Well, I'm nervous, even if nobody else is," Mike said, feeling a drop of sweat slide down his back.

And then it began. There seemed to be no cue, no ringleader, no spark to light the flame—nothing. One moment the fans were quiet, resting their voices from the first half. Then, as Allyssa and the other nominees for homecoming queen walked out onto the field, a rumble of voices began to boil up on all sides.

"Al-lys-sa!" the voices shouted. "Al-lys-sa! Al-lys-sa!"

Mike and Cindy looked around, bewildered.

Somewhere in the crowd, a friend of Allyssa's bounced up and down on her heels. "It's going to happen," she said softly to herself. "We've done it."

The girls, their escorts, and their families all stood near the center of the fifty-yard line as the crowd continued to scream Allyssa's name and stamp their feet.

The student council representative tasked with making the half-time announcements looked anxious as he stepped to the microphone. After a few opening remarks, he said, "Our Park Hill South homecoming queen for 2012 is . . ."

The young man paused a few beats. A hush fell across the audience like a blanket of heavy snow. The stadium sizzled with anticipation.

"Allyssa Brubeck!" he declared.

Mike and Cindy snapped their heads toward one another. The crowd erupted. Everyone was on their feet screaming and applauding. Allyssa jumped up and down, clapping her hands with unrestrained happiness.

The other contestants rushed to hug Allyssa, tears of joy streaming down their faces. Even the fans on the visitors' side rose to their feet to applaud the new homecoming queen.

As the crown was placed on her head, Allyssa glanced over at a select group of students seated along the front row. This was a win not only for Allyssa, but for them as well.

The kids dotting the front row were all members of the special education program at the school. Allyssa Brubeck is one of their classmates. Allyssa has Down syndrome.

Allyssa is also a marvel. Not only is she a genuinely happy person, she seems intent on raising the happiness level of everyone she encounters. Allyssa speaks to everyone she meets and hugs as many people as she can each day. She loves life and she loves people, and as a result, people love her.

Allyssa tried out for cheerleading, and although she can't do some of the more athletic routines, what she lacks in coordination and balance, she more than makes up for in passion and enthusiasm.

Ask any of her fellow students, and they'll tell you that Allyssa didn't receive the title because she is disabled. She won because they believe that she embodies true beauty and school spirit, and is therefore the perfect person to represent them.

As a result of Allyssa's coronation, local media featured her prominently for several days. However, this is not the first time Allyssa has been in the limelight.

A billboard campaign eliciting support for people with special needs featured Allyssa in her uniform, flanked by other cheerleaders from her school. The ad posed the question: "How do you treat someone with a disability?" And then it answered, "Just like everyone else!"

In many ways, Allyssa *is* just like everybody else. She goes to school, hangs out with her friends, she even works at a local bakery for a couple of hours every Saturday.

It's not Allyssa's disability that makes her special; it's her love of others. That—and she always seems to be smiling just a little bit more than most people.

Allyssa says that becoming happy isn't difficult. She offers these three suggestions for being a happy person.

1. **Hug people:** "When people are sad, I give them a hug," Allyssa says. "They feel better, and I feel good."

2. **Take an interest in other people:** When Mike and Cindy come home from work, Allyssa asks them questions showing genuine interest in their lives. She remembers her parents' friends and colleagues' names and never fails to ask how they are doing.

3. **Don't stress about it:** "People get worried all the time," Allyssa says. "That doesn't make things better. Stop worrying."

In Buddhism, a bodhisattva is an enlightened being who returns to Earth to teach human beings love and compassion. Perhaps Allyssa is a bodhisattva. One thing is for sure: she spreads joy wherever she goes.

HAPPY TO BE OF SERVICE

National Down Syndrome Society: www.NDSS.org

ACKNOWLEDGMENTS

Thank you to the happy individuals who allowed me to share their stories and their wisdom. You are bright lights, shining through the darkness of this world.

Thank you to Jeannine Becerra. Jeannine is one of the happiest people I know, and she has worked tirelessly by my side soliciting, interviewing for, organizing, and coordinating all of the stories you've read. Her collaboration on this project has been truly invaluable.

Thank you to Gary Krebs and all of my friends at Grand Harbor Press. Gary, you streamline my thoughts by polishing my words—you make me look good. You're a real mensch! To everyone else at Grand Harbor, you are fun, you are professional, and you continue to exceed my expectations.

Thank you to Steve Hanselman, my agent, friend, and collaborator. Together we continue to do great things for our world.

ABOUT THE AUTHOR

 Will Bowen was born in Manning, South Carolina, and grew up in Columbia, South Carolina. After a career in advertising sales and marketing, he became an ordained minister. He is the founder of A Complaint Free World, a nonprofit organization that has thus far touched the lives of more than ten million people in 106 countries. He is the author of the international bestseller *A Complaint Free World* and *Happy This Year!* (Grand Harbor Press). Will has been featured on *Oprah*, the *Today* show, The ABC World News, CBS Sunday Morning, *People* magazine, *Newsweek, The Wall Street Journal, O* magazine, *Chicken Soup for the Soul,* and more. Will maintains an active schedule speaking to organizations to help them eliminate workplace complaining and increase employee happiness, leading to greater productivity and profitability. Will is the proud father of Lia Bowen and currently lives in Kansas City, Missouri. His website is www.willbowen.com and his stand-alone site for *Happy This Year!* is www.happythisyear.com.

Kindle Serials

This book was originally released in Episodes as a Kindle Serial. Kindle Serials launched in 2012 as a new way to experience serialized books. Kindle Serials allow readers to enjoy the story as the author creates it, purchasing once and receiving all existing Episodes immediately, followed by future Episodes as they are published. To find out more about Kindle Serials and to see the current selection of Serials titles, visit www.amazon.com/kindleserials.